W9-CHY-665

Glass in the Modern World

A Study in Materials Development

F. J. Terence Maloney

Doubleday Science Series
Doubleday & Company, Inc.
Garden City, New York, 1968

First published in the United States of America in 1967 by Doubleday & Company,
Inc., Garden City, New York, in association with Aldus Books Limited
Library of Congress Catalog Card No. 67-10553
Copyright © Aldus Books Limited, London, 1967
Printed in Italy by Arnoldo Mondadori, Verona

Contents

Chapter 1 Glass is a Liquid   **9**

    Liquids and Solids   10
    The "Fourth State of Matter"   13
    Glass-Formers   18
    The Transformation Temperature   23

Chapter 2 The Properties of Glass   **29**

    Mechanical Properties   29
    Transparency   32
    Refraction   36
    Dispersion   38
    Chemical Stability   40
    Thermal Properties   41
    Electrical Properties   42
    Glass Types and Compositions   44

Chapter 3 The History of Glass   **49**

    Ancient Egyptian and Roman Glass   50
    The Middle Ages   54
    Venice and the European Revival   57
    Flat Glass up to the 19th Century   62
    English Lead-Crystal Glass   65
    Nineteenth-Century Glass   67

Chapter 4   Methods of Production   **73**

The Melting Process   73
Glass-Forming Processes   79
Blowing and Molding   79
Tube Drawing   87
Flat-Glass Manufacture   87
Glass Fiber Manufacture   94
Annealing   96
Toughened Glass   98
Laminated Safety Glass   100
Decorating Processes   103

Chapter 5   Optical Glass   **109**

Optical Problems and the Glassmaker   109
The History of Optical Glass   112
The Manufacture of Optical Glass   117
Making Lenses and Prisms   119
The Mechanism of Grinding and Polishing   124
Other Optical Uses of Glass   126

Chapter 6   Commercial and Industrial Glass   **129**

Glass Packaging   130
Glass in Building   135
Glass in Engineering   142
Electrical Uses   148
Domestic and Scientific Glassware   156

Chapter 7   New Kinds and Uses of Glass   **165**

Photosensitive Glass   166
Glass Ceramics   170
Chemically Toughened Glass   173
Photochromic Glass   175
Glass that Conducts Electrons   177
Fiber Optics   180
Glass in Modern Technology   185

Index   190

Suggested Reading

T. K. Derry and T. I. Williams, *A Short History of Technology*, Oxford University Press, Inc. (New York, 1961).

F. J. Gooding and E. Meigh (Editors), *Glass and W. E. S. Turner*, 1915-1951, (Society of Glass Technology, Sheffield, 1951).

F. Griffin, *Glass,* Soccer Associates (New Rochelle, New York, 1963).

L. Holland, *The Properties of Glass Surfaces*, John Wiley and Sons, Inc. (New York, 1964).

G. O. Jones, *Glass*, John Wiley and Sons, Inc. (New York, 1956).

J. D. Mackenzie (Ed.), *Modern Aspects of the Vitreous State*, Vols 1 and 3, Butterworth, Inc. (Washington, D.C., 1960, 1964).

P. W. McMillan, *Glass Ceramics*, Academic Press Inc. (New York, 1964).

B. E. Moody, *Packaging in Glass*, Hutchinson (London, 1963).

G. W. Morey, *The Properties of Glass*, Reinhold Publishing Corporation (New York, 1954).

L. M. Parr and C. A. Headley, *Laboratory Glass Blowing*, Tudor Publishing Company (New York, 1957).

C. J. Phillips, *Glass: Its Industrial Applications*, Reinhold Publishing Corporation (New York, 1960).

E. B. Shand, *Glass Engineering Handbook*, McGraw Hill (New York, 1958).

F. Twyman, *Prism and Lens Making*, Hilger and Watts (London, 1952).

W. A. Weyl and E. C. Marboe, *The Constitution of Glasses*, Vol 1, John Wiley and Sons, Inc. (New York, 1962).

Acknowledgments

Page 8 Reading University, photo J. A. Frost and J. Watkins: 12 Radio Times Hulton Picture Library: 28 Photo J. A. Frost and I. Maclean: 35 Photo K. Coton: 48 *Realites*, photo M. Desjardins: 50 (Left) British Museum, London (Right) Photo J. A. Frost: 52 (Top left, bottom right) British Museum, photo B. Kapadia (Top & center right) Smithsonian Institution: 53 (Left) British Museum (Right) Pilkington Brothers Ltd., St. Helens, England, photo B. Kapadia: 56 Victoria & Albert Museum, London: 57 Pilkington, photo B. Kapadia: 58 British Museum: 60 Pilkington, photo B. Kapadia: 61 Victoria & Albert Museum, photos K. Coton: 62-3 British Museum: 65 Saint-Gobain, France, photo Belzeauz-Raphò: 66 E. Barrington Haynes, *Glass Through the Ages*, Penguin Books Ltd., 1948: 67 United Glass Limited, England: 68 Pilkington, photo B. Kapadia: 69 Pilkington: 70 Royal Institute of British Architects: 72, 74 James A. Jobling & Co. Ltd., England: 76 Pilkington: 77 British Glass Industry Research Association: 80-1 Jobling: 82 United Glass: 84-5 (Bottom) Jobling: 85 (Top), 88 (Top) Glass Manufacturers' Federation, London: 88 (Bottom), 89,92-3 Pilkington: 96 United Glass: 101 Glass Manufacturers' Federation: 102 Triplex Safety Glass Company Limited, London: 105 (Top) Stuart & Sons Limited, Stourbridge, England (Bottom) Glass Manufacturers' Federation: 106 Pilkington: 128 Albright & Wilson Ltd: 132 Graham-Enock Mfg. Co. Ltd.: 133 Photos J. A. Frost and I. Maclean: 137 (Left) P.A.F. International (Right) Pilkington: 138 Fibreglass Limited, England: 140 Aluminium Federation, London: 141 Pilkington, photo B. Kapadia: 144 Triplex: 147 Fibreglass: 152 Glass Bulbs Ltd.: 153 General Electricity Generating Board, U.K.: 154 Corning Glass Works, New York, U.S.A.: 155 *Science Journal*, London: 156 Epsom Glass Industries Ltd., England: 157 I.C.I. Limited, Agricultural Division, U.K. and Q.V.F. Ltd., U.K.: 161 Jobling: 162 Camera Talks Ltd., London: 164 *Science Journal*: 167 *Industrial and Engineering Chemistry*, New York: 168 Corning: 170-1 *International Science and Technology*, New York: 172, 174 Corning: 176 *Science Journal*: 179 Mullard Research Laboratories: 180 Barr & Stroud Limited, Glasgow: 181 Jenaer Glaswerk Schott & Gin, Mainz: 184 (Top and center) Atomic Weapons Research Establishment, U.K., photo B. Kapadia (Bottom) Jenaer Glaswerk Schott: 186 Corning: 188 (Top) Barr & Stroud (Center) National Physical Laboratory, U.K., photo K. Coton (Bottom) Corning, photo K. Coton.

1 Glass is a Liquid

A glass is a rigid liquid. There is no inherent contradiction in this statement; rigidity is a matter of degree. To put it better, whether we see a particular liquid as fluid or rigid depends on the time scale of the experiment. All liquids, except the "superfluid" liquid helium, have some viscosity—that is, some stiffness or resistance to flow. If a mechanical stress is applied to a liquid more rapidly than the liquid can flow to relieve it, any liquid will behave like an elastic solid. At room temperature common glass is so viscous that its flow can be measured only with very delicate experiments, but it has the structure and indeed all the properties of a liquid if observed on a suitably expanded time scale. The familiar properties of glass result from this liquid structure.

The reader may feel that our talk of "experiments on a suitably expanded time scale" is mere pettifogging, and that we are obscuring a distinction (between liquid and solid) that is obvious to practical common sense. This is not the case. It is a common-

Partially devitrified glass (x 20)
viewed with polarized light. A line of
crystals has formed along the arc in
the center of the photograph; a group
of microscopic bubbles can be seen on
the right.

place that the viscosity of liquids increases as the temperature is lowered. The reluctance with which an automobile engine starts on a cold morning is usually due to the high viscosity of the cold engine oil. Most liquids, however, do not remain liquids at temperatures where they would become as viscous as glass. At a particular temperature, depending upon the material, they "freeze," that is, they undergo a distinct, discontinuous change of state from liquid to solid, as when liquid water freezes to ice. No such change occurs as a glass is cooled; the liquid simply becomes more and more viscous until it is as "stiff" as an ordinary solid.

The liquid from which glass is formed *may* freeze; under certain circumstances it may crystallize into a perfectly normal solid. When this happens, the material is said to have *devitrified*, and the product is no longer a glass. The temperature at which devitrification is most likely is just below the temperatures at which the materials melt. For common glass this temperature is around 1000°C. At room temperature, devitrification is unlikely because, paradoxically, the material is now too cold. We shall see later that a precise meaning can be given to these qualitative, somewhat vague statements. As a beginning, however, we shall state the definition: *A glass is a liquid that has become too cold to freeze.*

Liquids and Solids

Water is normally a "well-behaved" substance and the change of state from liquid water to ice is easy to study. At the freezing point of water, liquid water and ice may exist together (at the same temperature) but with quite different physical properties. In the liquid the individual water molecules are joined one to another, but not in any extended three-dimensional pattern. Further, some of the interatomic bonds joining the water molecules are constantly being broken, and new bonds formed, so that the liquid can flow. In the solid form (ice) the molecules take up an orderly spatial pattern, or crystal structure, as shown in the diagram. The bonds joining these molecules are rarely broken, and if they are broken, they are very likely to re-form as before. Most solid materials exhibit such a regular crystalline structure, but glass does not. The internal structure of glass is the random,

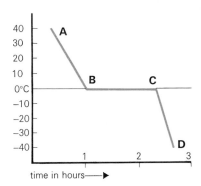

Temperature of water plotted against time for constant rate of heat extraction. From B to C, temperature is steady at the freezing point, although heat is being extracted as the liquid water turns to ice.

disordered structure that is normally seen in ordinary liquids.

We can get some insight into the nature of the change from liquid to solid by studying the temperature of a container of water, as we remove heat from the water at a constant rate. Imagine an apparatus in which a given volume of water is cooled by a flow of chilled brine at $-10°C$, that is, $10°C$ below the freezing point of water. In such an apparatus we can measure the amount of heat taken out of the water by measuring the temperature rise of the brine as it flows around the container. Heat energy is measured in calories; one calorie is the amount of heat required to raise a gram of liquid water by one centigrade degree, or, as in our experiment, lost by one gram of liquid water as it cools $1°C$. We can suppose our apparatus is automatically controlled to remove heat from the water at the rate of 100 calories per minute.

If we start with water well above its freezing point, we shall see that the temperature of the water falls steadily as heat is removed. Indeed, if we have 100 grams of water in our container, the temperature will fall at the rate of $1°C$ per minute (from the definition of a calorie). When the water reaches the freezing point, $0°C$, however, the temperature will remain stationary for a time, although we are still extracting heat—the brine is still being heated as it flows around the container. The temperature will remain at $0°C$ until all the water has turned to ice, and this process, in our apparatus, will take about 80 minutes; we shall have to extract 80 calories of heat energy to turn a gram of water

The regular patterns shown by snow-flakes (ice crystals) reflect the orderly arrangement of the water molecules in the normal solid state.

at 0°c into a gram of ice at 0°c. When all the water has turned to ice, the temperature will again begin to fall at a steady rate, but rather more rapidly than before. The *specific heat*—the amount of energy necessary to change the temperature of one gram of the material 1°c—is different for ice and for liquid water.

The heat energy we have been discussing appears physically as motion of the water molecules or of their constituent atoms. In ice, this motion is vibratory; the atoms vibrate around their fixed position in the crystal. In the liquid water, these vibratory motions continue, but additional motion of complete atoms or molecules from one position to another also occurs. The heat energy (80 calories per gram) necessary to melt ice at 0°c to water at 0°c is the energy that must be added to dissolve the fixed bonds of the crystal and bring about this additional motion. Conversely, this same amount of heat energy, called the *heat of fusion*, must be carried away for the liquid water to become ice.

For water, then, the change from liquid to solid is a distinct, discontinuous change. The gross physical properties of liquid water and ice are quite different: There is a discontinuous change in the specific heat (from 1 calorie per gram per degree for liquid water to about half that amount for ice); the change takes place at a definite temperature (under fixed conditions); and a definite amount of energy is released or required to bring about the change, with no change in temperature. The physical basis for all of these changes is the transition from the regular ordered crystal structure of ice to the disordered random structure of liquid water.

At sufficiently high temperatures glass flows as readily as water; at ordinary room temperature glass is as rigid and apparently solid as ice. However, as we cool the glass from the elevated temperatures to room temperature, we see none of the discontinuous changes that we observe when water freezes. As the glass cools, it simply flows less and less readily, until it becomes, for all practical purposes, a rigid material, effectively a "solid." But it still has the internal structure of a liquid. Since ordinary glass is a liquid cooled far below the point at which the material can, and sometimes does, crystallize, it is a *supercooled* liquid—that is, a liquid that has been cooled below its theoretical freezing point, while still retaining the properties and internal structure of a liquid.

The "Fourth State of Matter"

If one has very pure water, and is very careful, and has good luck as well, it is possible to supercool the water well below its normal freezing point without the formation of ice. There is no discontinuous change in the properties of the water as it passes the normal freezing point; the temperature falls steadily, no heat of fusion is liberated, and there is no change in the internal structure. The supercooled water is unstable, however—that is, it contains, as liquid water, more heat energy than is appropriate for the temperature. There is an alternative arrangement of the same molecules that is stable at that temperature and that contains less internal energy. This alternative arrangement is, of course, ice. If we drop a small crystal of ice into a container of water supercooled to $-10°$c, for example, the supercooled water will immediately turn to ice, until enough ice has been formed to raise the temperature (by the liberation of heat of fusion) to the normal freezing point of water, $0°$c.

Why were we able to supercool the water in the first place? For that matter, why can we supercool any liquid? In particular, why are we able to supercool liquid glass? There are several reasons that account for supercooling. A supercooled liquid is in what is called a *metastable* state. The basic principle involved

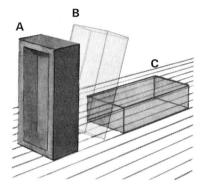

Metastable (A), unstable (B), and stable (C) states of a brick. State A is metastable because it can reach a lower energy state (C) only by passing through a state of higher energy.

is that, if several states are possible for a physical system, the most stable state is the one in which the energy of the system is the least. Water tends to run downhill, and the leaning tower of Pisa will fall down one day. But this basic principle only gives the expected end result, and does not tell us how or when that result will be achieved. It may be that the system can reach the state of lowest energy only by passing through an intermediate unstable state of higher energy than its present state. In that case, the present state is said to be metastable. The leaning tower is a particularly good example of a system in a metastable state. It could reach a more stable state and release a great deal of energy by falling over, but to fall over it needs a little more energy, in the form of an initial push.

The molecules of a supercooled liquid are in much the same condition as the leaning tower. There are intermolecular bonds between the molecules of the liquid, and for the crystal to form, these bonds must be broken and new bonds formed in the regular crystal pattern. The end result will be a lower overall energy for the system, but the individual molecules do not take such a broad view of the situation. For a molecule to release its bond in the liquid configuration, a certain minimum of energy must be made available. This energy can be "repaid" with ample interest when the same molecule assumes a much less energetic bond in the crystal, but the initial push or activation energy must be available to cross the energy hump. If the liquid involved is very

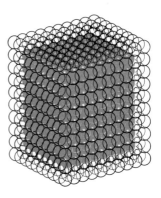

In the smallest crystal shown, all 8 atoms are on the surface; in the next size, 1 out of the 27 occupies an internal position; in the largest (still a very small crystal), a little over half the atoms are internal.

viscous, the necessary *activation energy* per bond may be quite high, so that the liquid can remain in the metastable supercooled state for some time.

Another matter involved is the relative instability of very small crystals. To calculate the internal energy of a system containing both the liquid and solid phase of the material concerned, such as a mixture of liquid water and ice, one must consider the energy of the liquid, the energy of the solid, and the energy of the interface, or boundary between the solid and the liquid. The energy of a molecule on the boundary, or surface, of the crystal may be higher than that of a molecule in the liquid, or inside the crystal. For a system containing large crystals, this surface energy is negligible, in comparison with the total energy in the liquid and solid phases. But a very small crystal has a high proportion of its molecules on the surface, and thus in a high energy state. For example, the simplest cubic crystal, with two molecules along each edge, would contain a total of eight molecules, and all would be on the surface. The next size larger, with three molecules along an edge, would have only one of its 27 molecules inside. By contrast, a cubic crystal with 1000 molecules along each edge would have over 99.9 per cent of its molecules in interior positions. The result is that very small crystals have lower melting points than do larger crystals. For crystals large enough to be visible, this effect is negligible, but for very small crystals it can be important. And if crystals are to form in a pure liquid as it is cooling they must start as very small crystals. A liquid is said to be supercooled if it is cooled below the melting point of large crystals; but if there is no way for these crystals to get started, the liquid may be supercooled some distance below this theoretical freezing point before crystallization begins.

A seed crystal of the same material, such as our piece of ice dropped into supercooled water, is the most potent starter or *nucleating agent* for crystallization, but many kinds of crystalline materials will serve almost as well. Ordinarily, water contains enough microscopic solid impurities to serve as nucleating agents, so that we rarely see supercooled water occurring naturally. However, droplets of water supercooled by as much as 40°C are found in clouds, presumably because the water is very pure and there is no way for the crystallization process to start.

In the case of glass, the relative instability of very small crystals helps in cooling the glass below the freezing point of the material concerned, but when the glass is grossly supercooled, as glass is at room temperature, it is the first mechanism we discussed—the difficulty of dissolving the intermolecular bonds of the liquid configuration—that accounts for the failure of the glass to crystallize. In some applications, one deliberately causes crystals to form in glass, but to do this the glass must be heated to a temperature just below the melting point of the crystals concerned, or the process will occur too slowly to be of practical interest.

The molecules of a liquid, then, are not independent of one another, but are joined by intermolecular bonds, although in a disorderly or random pattern. For a liquid to flow, there must be a constant breaking and re-forming of these intermolecular bonds, and the viscosity, or resistance to flow, of the liquid is (inversely) a measure of the readiness with which these rearrangements can take place. Viscosity is measured in *poises*—for example, liquid water has a viscosity of about 0.01 poise at 20°C; the viscosity increases to about 0.018 poise at 0°C, and to over 0.025 poise if the water is supercooled to –9°C. Light machine oil has a viscosity of about one poise unit at room temperature; heavy machine oil about 6 poises at room temperature; glycerin about 200 poises. At room temperature ordinary glass has a viscosity

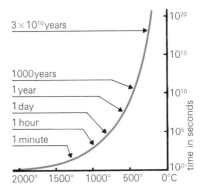

Comparison of times for a standard deformation by viscous flow in glass. The deformation that requires 1 second at 1800°C or 1 minute at 1300°C requires over 30 thousand million years at room temperature.

of approximately 10^{20} poise units (that is, 10 followed by 19 zeros). Given sufficient time, glass would do all the things we expect of an ordinary liquid. The viscosity of glass at room temperature is so high, however, that the time involved would be measured in thousands of millions of years.

It has been proposed that supercooled liquids, and in particular glassy materials, should be considered a "fourth state of matter," in addition to the solid, liquid, and gaseous states normally discussed. But this proposal overstates the case; glass is a perfectly ordinary liquid, exceptional only because its viscosity is so high that its flow properties show only on an enormously expanded time scale. Many of the other properties of glass (or other liquids) do not involve flow, however, and in these properties, which we shall discuss shortly, glass behaves as a perfectly normal liquid and is most easily understood as a liquid.

The justification of our definition of glass as "a liquid that has become too cold to freeze" should now be clear. The materials of which glass is formed can and do freeze (that is, crystallize into normal solids) under appropriate circumstances. However, if they are cooled far below the temperature at which they would normally crystallize, the viscosity of the liquid becomes so high that the internal rearrangements necessary for crystallization can no longer take place—the liquid has become too cold to freeze. In order to distinguish glasses, which become so viscous that they are, for practical purposes, rigid solids, from simply supercooled liquids, a viscosity of 10^{13} poises is sometimes specified as the minimum stiffness a supercooled liquid must reach before it is considered a glass. A material with a viscosity less than this minimum would deform under its own weight in a short time, but this is not the only reason for proposing this minimum viscosity for a glass. While glasses do not crystallize, they do undergo another type of freezing peculiar to glass, as we shall see later. This peculiar type of freezing occurs when the viscosity of the material reaches approximately 10^{13} poises. Before we discuss this and other properties of glass, however, we must consider some of the kinds of materials that are particularly susceptible to supercooling, and so are likely to form glasses.

Glass-formers

A surprisingly large number of materials can be obtained as glasses under special conditions. It is even possible to obtain water in the form of glass, if it is cooled sufficiently rapidly, although the experiment is not easy to carry out. If the water has a large amount of some other material in solution, it is easier to obtain the glassy form of water with rapid cooling, since the atoms or ions of solute interfere with the crystallization process, and allow the temperature to fall to the point where the viscosity of the water becomes so high that crystal (ice) formation is difficult. In this connection it is known that simple living organisms (tadpoles, for example) will survive temperatures as low as $-90°C$ if they are brought to this temperature rapidly, so that the formation of ice crystals in the tissue is avoided. It may be that in these cases, the water in the organisms enters the glassy state without the discontinuous and harmful change of physical properties entailed in ice formation.

The great bulk of common glasses are based on silicon dioxide, SiO_2, as the parent glass-former. Silicon dioxide occurs abundantly in nature in pure crystalline form as quartz and cristobalite, and as a component of numerous silicate minerals. Most common sand contains a high proportion of SiO_2. The pure crystalline forms of silicon dioxide have melting points around 1700°C, so that pure SiO_2 glass is supercooled by almost 1700°C.

The formula SiO_2 hardly conveys the nature of silicon dioxide.

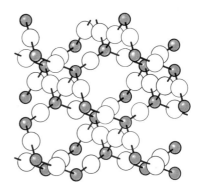

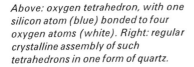

Above: oxygen tetrahedron, with one silicon atom (blue) bonded to four oxygen atoms (white). Right: regular crystalline assembly of such tetrahedrons in one form of quartz.

Actually, each silicon atom is bonded to four oxygen atoms, and each oxygen atom is shared between two silicon atoms. The resulting structure for one form of quartz is shown in the accompanying diagram. Each silicon atom is shown at the center of a tetrahedron. The angle between the four bonds in which each silicon atom participates is fixed (108°) in both crystalline silica and silica glass. The angle between the two bonds of each oxygen atom is not as critical, however, so that the oxygen atoms joining two tetrahedrons provide the flexibility necessary for the amorphous structure of glass.

It is difficult to represent the nature of the structure possible with these SiO_2 tetrahedrons, and similar figures, in two-dimensional diagrams, as the reader will probably be prepared to grant from inspecting the diagram given. We can make use of the device proposed by Warren and Zachariasen and consider an imaginary two-dimensional element, G (for glass-former), that forms an oxide G_2O_3 in two dimensions only. The SiO_2 tetrahedrons, with oxygen atoms at the four corners, are replaced in our two-dimensional systems by oxygen triangles, with oxygen at the corners and the atom of our imaginary element G in the center of the triangle. The reader must then imagine the argument extended to three dimensions. The regular crystalline form of our two-dimensional oxide, G_2O_3, and the amorphous disordered form found in the liquid (and thus in the glass) are both shown in the diagram. Note that in either form the number of bonds per

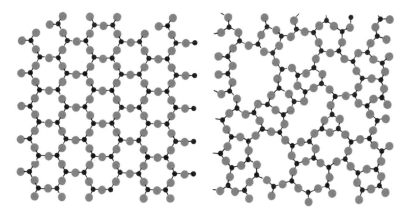

Left: regular crystalline form of imaginary two-dimensional oxide, G_2O_3
Right: amorphous or glassy form of G_2O_3. (Oxygen atoms shown in red.)

atom is the same, and that the structure is quite an "open" one with a good deal of unoccupied space. In the amorphous, or glassy form, the bond angles are slightly distorted from the 60° and 180° angles seen in the hypothetical crystalline form.

Pure SiO_2 glass, known as "fused quartz" or "fused silica," is used for critical applications, but has too high a softening temperature for general purposes. At the temperature necessary to melt quartz sand, 1700°C, the liquid SiO_2 is quite viscous, and by the time the liquid SiO_2 has been supercooled to 1300°C the viscosity is already in the neighborhood of 10^{12} poises, far too stiff for convenient shaping by blowing or drawing. The addition of certain metallic oxides, such as soda (Na_2O) and lime (CaO), to the SiO_2 lowers the viscosity (and the temperature required to melt the materials initially) to more practical levels. Glass is normally worked at viscosities of 10^3 to 10^6 poises, and for commercial soda-lime-silica glass the required temperature is only 600–700°C.

The reason that the addition of the metallic oxides lowers the viscosity can be seen in the diagram, where we again use our imaginary two-dimensional glass, G_2O_3, now with the addition of a metallic ion, M, introduced as an oxide, M_2O. The metal ion occupies the space in the formerly open G_2O_3 network, and it

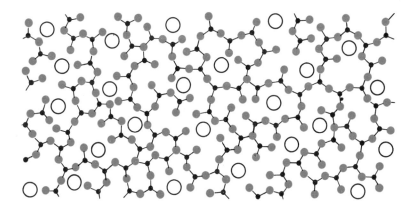

Imaginary two-dimensional glass, G_2O_3, modified by addition of metallic ions (large white circles).

would appear that this would stiffen the structure. However, each metallic ion removes one of the bonds of an oxygen atom from the basic G_2O_3 network, or, in real glass, from the SiO_2 network. Furthermore, the bond between the metallic ion and the oxygen atom is essentially nondirectional. The result is that the structure is less well braced with the metallic ions present, and therefore is less stiff or viscous.

Silicon dioxide exemplifies the primary characteristics a glass-former must possess. First, the fact that each oxygen atom is shared between two silicon atoms, and each silicon atom between four oxygen atoms allows the formation of complex three-dimensional networks. Second, the silicon-oxygen bond is a very strong bond. The result is that it is very difficult to disentangle the network in its amorphous liquid form to permit the formation of crystals. The diagram of the structure of quartz on page 19 shows an orderly crystalline arrangement of SiO_2. If the reader will consider that diagram along with the diagram of our imaginary two-dimensional glass G_2O_3 on page 20, he will be able to imagine how complex is the structure of SiO_2 in the liquid or glassy form.

In addition to silicon, there are a number of other elements whose oxides, sulfides, tellurides, and selenides form inorganic glasses. Boron, germanium, phosphorus, vanadium, arsenic, and zirconium are examples. Beyond these primary glass-formers there are the so-called intermediates, titanium, zinc, lead, aluminum, thorium, beryllium, and cadmium, whose oxides do not form glasses alone, but may take part in a glass network with one of the primary glass-formers. Both the primary glass-formers and the intermediates form strongly directional bonds that stiffen the glass structure. Beyond these are a number of modifiers, such as the Na_2O and CaO mentioned previously, whose presence does not contribute to the network strength as such, and serves usually to lower the viscosity of glass as well as contributing desirable chemical, optical, or indeed economic properties to the basic glass. The bond strength decreases regularly as one passes from primary glass-formers through intermediates to modifiers.

The oxide glasses are usually opaque to radiation in the infrared portion of the electromagnetic spectrum, and, for infrared work, the sulfides, tellurides, and selenides of arsenic have become quite important. Arsenic trisulfide, for example, forms a glass that is opaque to visible light, but transparent in the infrared region. Pure SiO_2 transmits light in the ultraviolet region, but the addition of almost any of the common modifiers will render the glass opaque to ultraviolet light, and, because of the high melting point of SiO_2, the formation of pure SiO_2 glass for ultraviolet lenses is a matter of considerable difficulty.

At least one elemental glass—that is, a glass formed of a single element rather than a compound—is known. Liquid sulfur, if cooled very rapidly, becomes a rubbery, elastic "glass" at room temperature. This "glass" is only moderately stable, and devitrifies fairly rapidly, however. Among organic compounds, the carbon-to-carbon linkage furnishes the basis for network formation, and many of the common plastics, particularly the transparent plastics such as Lucite or Perspex, are technically speaking glasses. In this book, however, we shall follow the common usage of the term *glass* and treat only the inorganic glasses, particularly the oxide glasses based on silicon.

The Transformation Temperature

We said that although glass did not crystallize (or if it did, it would not formally be glass) it did undergo a peculiar type of freezing. This peculiar type of freezing is of very great importance in glass technology, as well as in the theoretical understanding of glass. The effect of this "freezing" is not to alter the structure of the glass, but to change the way it expands and contracts with changes in temperature.

We have seen that the heat energy in a liquid or a solid appears as motion of the atoms or molecules of the material. In a crystalline solid, the molecules occupy fixed positions relative to one another, and the molecular motions are vibratory motions around this fixed position. In a liquid, these vibratory motions occur, but there is some random movement of the molecules so that some intermolecular bonds are constantly being dissolved and new bonds formed. In both liquids and solids, part of the vibratory motion due to heat is motion along the axis of the interatomic bonds in the material, so that the distance between two neighboring atoms varies slightly as these atoms vibrate. In general, the higher the temperature, the greater the amplitude of the vibrations.

Interatomic bonds may be formed in a number of different ways, but always involve a balance of attractive and repulsive forces. At the normal interatomic spacing, these forces balance and the net force between the two atomic nuclei is zero. It is almost always true, however, that at this normal interatomic spacing it is easier to pull the two atoms a little further apart than to compress them further together. The result is that the thermal vibration has the effect of slightly increasing the interatomic spacing. Therefore, most materials expand slightly as the temperature rises, and correspondingly contract as it falls. This normal thermal expansion involves no rearrangement of interatomic or intermolecular bonds, but merely changes the effective average spacing between atoms.

Glass undergoes normal thermal expansion and contraction, but, at above a temperature called the *transformation temperature*, it undergoes a second kind of expansion or contraction as the temperature changes. We saw earlier (page 10) that glass has an "open" structure; the network of silicon and oxygen atoms (in a common glass) is not densely packed. As the temperature decreases, however, the structure becomes more dense. Consider a ring of eight silicon atoms alternating with eight oxygen atoms. Each of the silicon atoms in this ring is bonded, through oxygen atoms, to two silicon atoms not in the ring. At a high temperature, this configuration may be stable. At a lower temperature, two of the silicon atoms in the ring may release one of their bonds outside the ring, and, with an intervening oxygen atom, form a bridge across the center of the ring. The entire ring will now have a less open structure and occupy less space. This description of *configurational shrinkage* is greatly oversimplified; the important point is that configurational expansion or contraction involves rearrangement of interatomic bonds and therefore is quite different from normal thermal expansion previously described.

The way the volume of a given weight of glass varies as the glass is cooled is shown in the diagram opposite. Beginning at A with the glass as a normal liquid (that is, above the melting point of the glass-forming materials) we cool the liquid to B, the theoretical freezing point. If the material crystallizes there will be a sharp decrease in volume to C, after which the crystalline material will continue to shrink as temperature falls, but at a slower rate (per degree of cooling), to D, the volume at room temperature. From A to B, the liquid has contracted by two methods, normal thermal contraction and the configurational contraction due to assuming a less open structure. From C to D, the crystal, which undergoes no configurational change, shrinks only by normal thermal contraction. (We should mention here that most materials shrink on crystallizing. The increase in volume when ice is formed from liquid water is the exception, not the rule.)

If we avoid crystallization and are able to supercool the liquid, the supercooled liquid continues to shrink at the same rate, per degree of temperature decrease, as did the normal liquid. Both kinds of shrinkage are still occurring from A to E. At a particular point, however, the rate of contraction slows, and below that point continues from E to F at the rate previously discussed for the crystal. Apparently, the configurational shrink-

25

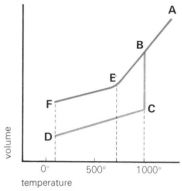

Changes in glass volume on cooling. The line *ABCD* represents a substance that crystallizes at *B*; the line *ABEF* the glassy form of the same material.

age has stopped at E, and, from E to F, the glass, although still a liquid, is shrinking only by normal thermal contraction. The temperature at which this occurs (the transformation temperature) is not a sharply defined point, but rather a range of about 50°C, as the bend in the curve suggests.

What happens at the transformation temperature is that the glass has become so viscous that the configurational changes necessary for the denser structure no longer have time to occur. These changes involve rearrangement of the intermolecular bonds, and when the glass has reached a particular viscosity, the necessary changes can no longer keep pace with the rate at which the temperature is falling. The interesting point is that the viscosity at which this occurs, for practical cooling rates, is roughly the same for all glasses, 10^{13} poises, although the temperature involved may range from −89°C for glycerin to over 1000°C for pure silica glass. The fact that the configurational shrinkage ceases at this viscosity is the reason for making a viscosity of 10^{13} poises the formal borderline between a glass and a simple supercooled liquid.

The term "transformation temperature" is a bit of a misnomer, in that the glass undergoes no transformation at this temperature; what happens is that, for practical purposes, it ceases to undergo the internal transformations appropriate to its actual temperature. Further, the configurational changes do not actually cease. They simply continue at the rate set by the viscosity of the glass. The point is that when this viscosity has reached the

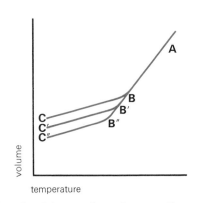

Effect of cooling rate on final glass volume. A rapidly cooled glass will follow the line ABC; in a glass cooled more slowly the configurational shrinkage can keep pace with the cooling to a lower temperature (B") and the glass will occupy a smaller volume (C") at room temperature.

region of 10^{13} poises the rate involved is so slow that cooling rates will cause the configurational changes to fall behind the temperature change, and when the glass reaches room temperature and a viscosity of 10^{20} poises, the change has, for practical purposes, stopped altogether.

There are, in fact, two properties of a glass that do change at the transformation temperature. The first is the rate of thermal expansion, as already discussed. The second, reasonably enough, is the specific heat of the glass—that is, the amount of heat energy required to raise the temperature of one gram of glass 1°C. Below the transformation temperature, all the heat supplied goes into the molecular vibrations only, as no appreciable configurational change is occurring; above the transformation temperature the individual molecules can also move about somewhat in the material, and some of the heat energy goes into this motion as well as into the vibratory motion of the molecules. Accordingly, the specific heat may increase appreciably as the transformation temperature is exceeded.

The temperature at which a particular piece of glass, on being cooled, effectively ceases to undergo configurational change, is sometimes called the *fictive temperature* of the glass. This is the temperature at which the glass would be thermodynamically stable—that is, would have no spontaneous tendency to change to a more dense or less dense structure. The fictive temperature of common glass is in the neighborhood of 500°C, and it follows that the glass is not in thermodynamic equilibrium at room temperature. Common glass is, in principle, unstable at room temperature. It is, in fact, slowly shrinking, because the configurational change will continue until the fictive temperature reaches the actual temperature. For glass at room temperature, however, the process goes forward so slowly that millions of years would be required.

Since rates (of cooling and of configurational shrinkage) are involved, it would seem that the temperature at which this transformation occurs should depend on the rate of cooling. This is indeed the case. As shown in the diagram, if the cooling rate is high, the configurational change falls behind at a higher temperature; if it is very slow, the transformation temperature is correspondingly lower. We may thus obtain glass of the same composition, but of different densities—that is, different fictive temperatures—according to the rate at which the glass is cooled. Also, within the same piece of glass, the density may vary if the exterior part of the glass has cooled more rapidly than the interior. Finally, the glass may change in dimensions after it has cooled, due to continued configurational shrinkage. The effect is ordinarily negligible, but in certain applications, such as precision thermometers, it can be a nuisance. We shall refer later to the use made of the different densities obtained by different cooling rates within the same piece of glass in the manufacture of "toughened" glass.

We may now restate our definition of a glass in somewhat more formal terms. A glass is a material obtained by supercooling a liquid to a temperature where the viscosity of the liquid exceeds 10^{13} poises, but without incurring discontinuous changes in viscosity or structure, the material retaining the organization and internal structure of a liquid. As the preceding discussion has implied, cooling beyond the temperature where this viscosity is reached will have little effect on the internal structure of the material, except to increase the viscosity further; the viscosity of common glass at room temperature exceeds 10^{20} poises, and the material behaves, over the time periods of interest to people, as an ideal elastic solid.

2   The Properties of Glass

Although glasses may be formed of a number of different materials with correspondingly different properties, many of the most common properties of glass are direct consequences of the glassy state. In this chapter we shall see how such properties arise from that state.

Mechanical Properties

On a practical human time scale, stresses are usually applied and results measured at a rate far too fast for the flow properties of glass at room temperature to show. Under these circumstances common glass behaves like an elastic solid. In bulk, glass appears almost completely rigid, but in thin sheets or fibers it is quite pliable, provided that the radius of curvature is large compared to the thickness of the glass.

We saw in Chapter 1 that the silicon-oxygen bond was very strong, so that glass should be a very strong material. In principle this is true. Newly formed fine glass fibers will support loads of

A strain pattern in glass, the result
of an applied mechanical stress,
revealed by using polarized light.

well over 70,000 kg/cm² (1 kilogram per square centimeter is roughly 14 pounds to the square inch). This figure is five times that obtained by our best steels; and, more important, it is twice as much as steel could support even in theory. The practical strength of materials, however, is greatly affected by defects and irregularities. Such defects, particularly surface defects that lead to cracks, make the actual strength of ordinary glass less than one hundredth of the theoretical value calculated from the strength of the interatomic bonds.

Since glass is effectively rigid, an applied force will be concentrated, by the leverage involved, on the few intermolecular bonds at the base of a small surface crack. Although these bonds are very strong, the rigidity of the glass allows what amount to macroscopic forces to be applied to a few submicroscopic structures, and the bonds, strong or weak, must give way. Because a glass has the homogenous structure of a liquid, a crack, once begun, encounters no internal boundaries or discontinuities to interrupt its progress. Further, as the crack deepens, the effective leverage increases and the fracturing of further bonds becomes that much easier. The crack therefore spreads rapidly across the entire piece of glass.

The crack sensitivity of glass is such that glass is weak in tension, although very strong in compression, where stresses do not lead to cracks. To increase the useful strength of glass, at least three courses are open: One may attempt to prevent surface defects that allow cracks to start; one may try to avoid ever putting the glass surface in tension; or finally, one may attempt to prevent a crack from spreading. All these techniques have been used. It is not very profitable to try to prevent minute cracks in an exposed glass surface, but one may protect the glass surface with a tough skin of another material. The skin then protects the glass against chemical as well as mechanical attack. This is the basis of the "Titanizing" process to be described in Chapter 6.

The troublesome cracks originate from surface defects, and spread to the interior if the glass surface is placed in tension. The second method of strengthening glass mentioned above is to avoid placing the surface in tension. Although it seems a bit

A

The principle of thermal glass toughening. The shrunken inner portion in diagram B places the surface layers in permanent compression.

B

magical, there are at least two ways in which this can be done: by thermal and chemical "toughening." In thermal toughening, the piece to be toughened is heated above its transformation temperature, and the surface is then rapidly chilled. The configurational shrinkage of the surface is thus arrested, but the interior, not yet cooled, undergoes further configurational shrinkage. When the entire piece is cool, the interior is permanently in tension, and the surface permanently in compression. A similar result can be obtained by placing the hot glass article in contact with a salt that will exchange large metallic ions for smaller ones from the surface of the glass. For example, if a glass containing lithium (Li^+) is brought into contact with sodium chloride ($NaCl$) under appropriate conditions, some of the Li^+ ions near the surface of the glass will be replaced by Na^+ ions, on a one-for-one basis. The Na^+ ions are larger than the Li^+ ions they replace, so, when the glass cools, the surface cannot shrink as much as does the interior. Before a crack can begin in toughened glass the piece must be bent far enough to overcome the surface compression and place the surface in tension. Such glasses may have impact strength four to ten times as great as that of untoughened glass.

The final technique for strengthening glass is to provide a way of stopping a crack from spreading. If glass fibers are embedded in a matrix of suitable resin that, though weaker than the glass, can deform to distribute a stress, a crack across a single fiber will not seriously weaken the material. The load is transferred to the remaining fibers by the matrix, and, indeed, to the portions

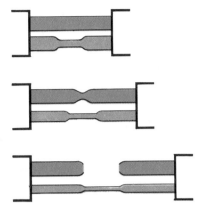

When drawn, metals (brown) "neck" and break; glass (blue) flows like a theoretical liquid and does not neck, even if originally of nonuniform cross section.

of the broken' fiber remaining intact. The crack that in the fiber resin system destroys only a small part of one fiber would in bulk glass have spread over the entire piece. The "glass ceramics" to be discussed in Chapter 7 represent a related strategy. Crystals are deliberately formed in the glass—that is, it is partially devitrified to provide discontinuities, and therefore barriers to crack propagation.

In discussing the mechanical properties of glass, we must point out that the drawing (and related techniques such as blowing) of glass depends on its behaving as a proper theoretical liquid. Strain (deformation) of a viscous liquid is directly proportional to the applied stress. When glass is drawn it does not "neck" or develop weak spots as, for example, metals do. The contrasting behavior of hot metal and hot glass is shown in the diagram.

Transparency

The reader will not be surprised to learn that the transparency of glass derives from its basic liquid structure. It is common for liquids to be transparent, while transparency is relatively rare in solids. Not all liquids, and indeed not all glasses, are transparent, however, and we must show how transparent glass differs from opaque liquids. To explain this point, we must say a little about the nature of light.

We may think of light as particulate (that is, composed of a stream of discrete packets of energy, called *photons*) or as a wave phenomenon. In modern theory the two descriptions are completely equivalent. For the moment we are interested in light as a stream of photons. There is a particular amount of energy carried by each photon. When light falls on a bulk metal, the energy of each photon is absorbed and as promptly re-radiated by "free" electrons within the metal. These electrons are free in the sense that they can absorb or release energy over a wide range, in particular over the range required to absorb and then re-radiate light. Therefore the metal reflects light falling on its surface. In typical glasses, the electrons are not free in this sense; they are bound quite rigidly to particular energy levels, and the metallic kind of reflection does not occur.

But glass does absorb light of particular wavelengths—that is, particular colors of light. Common glass is, in fact, opaque to wavelengths at the infrared and ultraviolet ends of the spectrum for this reason. We referred in Chapter 1 to the kinds of molecular vibrations possible in a material that do not involve any permanent change of position of the molecules. These vibrating systems are "tuned" systems—that is, they can vibrate only at certain specific frequencies or modes of vibration, although each system may have several of these allowable frequencies. There is a definite amount of energy per photon, increasing as the wavelength of the light decreases—that is, photons of violet light contain more energy than do photons of red light. It may be that a photon of light of a particular color may have just the right amount of energy to excite one of these vibrating systems from one mode of vibration to another, more energetic, mode. If so, photons of that frequency will be absorbed by the material, and the energy absorbed will not necessarily be re-radiated immediately or at the same frequency. The material will then absorb the particular color of light concerned.

It happens that the common glasses do not have energy systems that can accept the range of energies represented by photons of visible light, although they do absorb both infrared and ultraviolet radiation. The fact that common glass does not absorb light is due not to the inherent character of glass, but to careful selection of materials. Very small amounts of certain impurities will lead to tinted or virtually opaque glass. Iron oxide, yielding deep green and brown colors, is in practice the most troublesome impurity of this kind. Of course, appropriate "impurities" may be added deliberately when a tinted glass is especially required.

Common glass, then, does not reflect light in the metallic sense, nor does it absorb visible light. Except insofar as bulk metals are unlikely to form glasses (the type of interatomic bond that permits the free electrons in metal is not the type required to form glass), neither preconditions for transparency are necessary consequences of either the liquid or the glassy state. But there is more coming: The structure of a glass or of any liquid is irregular, and the individual molecules are much smaller than the wavelength of visible light. Thus there are in fact no structures large enough to obstruct the passage of a light wave. The wavelength of visible light is from roughly 4000 to 7000 angstrom units (one angstrom unit—that is, 1 A—is 10^{-8} centimeters or 0.00000001 cm.). The individual glass molecules are roughly 2 to 3 A in size. A light wave is no more obstructed by a single one of these molecules or by an irregularly spaced set of such structures than an ocean wave is obstructed by an individual pebble on a beach. To the light, the nonreflecting, nonabsorbing glass is simply "another kind of space."

The glass is distinctly *another* kind of space to the light, however. It is a space filled with charged particles, the electrons and protons that make up the individual atoms. Light is, after all, an electromagnetic disturbance in space, and the disturbance (that is, the light wave) does not travel as fast through a space filled with charged particles as through a vacuum. The ratio of the speed of light in a vacuum to its speed in glass (or any other transparent medium) is called the refractive index for the medium, and ranges from 1.5 to 1.9 for different kinds of common glass. Whenever light passes the boundary between media of different refractive indexes, as from air to glass, a certain amount of light is reflected at the boundary. The amount reflected depends on the difference in refractive index of the two media; for common glass about four per cent of the incident light is reflected at each air-glass boundary. The reflection is quite different from the metallic kind of total reflection discussed previously.

The stacks of glass plates, each 0.1 mm. thick, become increasingly opaque as more plates are added, due to reflection loss at each air-glass boundary. The two large piles contain 100 plates each; but the plates in the large pile on the right are cemented together with material with the same refractive index as glass, eliminating the internal optical boundaries, and making the pile transparent.

We come now to the crux of our argument. A liquid, including a glass, has no internal boundaries or discontinuities. We have spoken loosely of individual glass molecules, but we could perfectly well view the whole of a piece of glass as one large molecule. Accordingly, as light passes completely through a piece of glass, it encounters only two optical boundaries, the first one on entering the glass and the second on leaving it. Eight to ten per cent of the light may be lost by reflection at these two boundaries, but almost all the rest passes safely through. It is rare for crystalline solids in bulk to possess this kind of internal homogeneity. A single perfect crystal may be quite transparent, but bulk solids are usually made up of millions of single crystals, and as light passes the boundaries of these crystals, some light is lost by reflection at each boundary, and the material is effectively opaque. It is thus the internal homogeneity of glass, which is typical of liquids but not of solids, that is the basis for the transparency of glass. The point is illustrated by the photograph on this page.

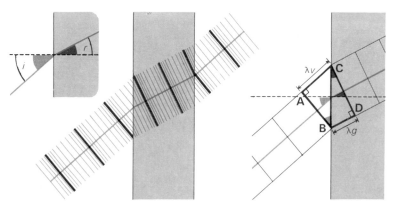

Refraction is the result of the difference between the velocity of light in a vacuum (v_v), and the velocity in glass (v_g). The direction of the ray is measured from the perpendicular to the vacuum-glass boundary, as shown at the left. Since the frequency of light is fixed (for a particular color) the wavelength—the distance the light travels during one cycle—depends directly on its velocity, and the wavelength in a vacuum, AC, is greater than that in the glass, BD. Since the wave fronts AB and CD are perpendicular to the ray, the line BC is the common hypotenuse of the right triangles ABC and BCD; hence the ratio sin i/sin r $=\lambda_v/\lambda_g$ $=v_v/v_g$ is the refractive index.

Refraction

We introduced the refractive index of a transparent medium as the speed of light in a vacuum (or the speed in air, which is practically the same) divided by its speed in the medium concerned. When a ray of light passes between two media in which it travels at different speeds, it undergoes a change in direction unless it encounters the boundary exactly at right angles. The reason can be seen in the diagram above. The effect of glass in bending (refracting) light was well known before it was realized that the relative speeds of light in glass and in air were involved.

In discussing refraction, the direction of the ray of light is measured from a line called the *normal*, which is perpendicular to the air-glass surface. The angle so measured, of the ray falling on the glass, is called the *angle of incidence* (i); the angle made by the refracted ray within the glass is called the *angle of refraction* (r). It was found empirically that for a given kind of glass the ratio sin i : sin r was the same for all values of i, and this ratio was

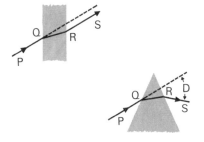

A ray of light passing through a parallel-sided glass block emerges parallel to its original path but displaced laterally from it. If the sides of the block are not parallel the ray is deviated through the angle D, called *the* angle of deviation. The path of a ray is reversible—that is, if a ray were traveling from right to left along SR, it would emerge traveling along QP.

called the *refractive index* (*n*) of the glass

$$n = \frac{\sin i}{\sin r}$$

The reader may satisfy himself by reference to the diagram that *n*, as just defined, is the same as the ratio of the speed of light in air to the speed in glass.

When a ray of light passes out into the air again its speed increases to its original value and its direction changes again, in the opposite sense to the change that occurred when it entered. If the sides of the glass slab are parallel to each other, the final direction of the light is parallel to its initial direction; the ray has been *displaced* but not *deviated*—or, more precisely, the deviations that it has suffered at each surface cancel each other out. If the glass does not have parallel sides, the ray will suffer a net deviation, as shown in the diagram above. This diagram also illustrates the fact that the path of a light ray through a system is reversible in the sense that it can be traced backward and still be consistent with the laws of refraction.

When a ray emerges from glass into air, it is bent away from the normal, as shown on page 38. It follows that as the angle *r* is made larger the angle *i* will eventually reach 90° so that the emergent ray is traveling parallel to the surface. For any larger value of *r*, refraction is impossible, and the ray is simply reflected inside the glass. This phenomenon is called *total internal reflection* ("total" as opposed to the partial reflection that always accompanies refraction). The value of *r* for which the changeover occurs is called the *critical angle*, and since sin 90°=1, its value

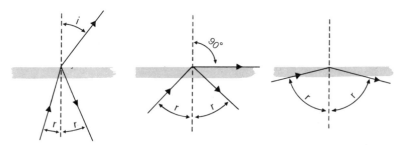

Total internal reflection. Light emerging from glass into air is refracted away from the normal (dotted line), and at the same time partial internal reflection occurs (left). When the angle r has its critical value, the emergent ray is parallel to the surface (center), and for values of r larger than this, total internal reflection occurs (right). (The letters i and r are used here to refer to the rays in air and glass respectively, and no longer stand for the words "incident" and "refracted." The equation sin i =n sin r still holds good.)

must be given by $\sin r = 1/n$. If $n = 1.50$, the critical value of r is about 42°. We shall see in Chapter 7 how total internal reflection is exploited in the field of fiber optics.

Dispersion

The fact that a prism of glass, or of any transparent material, will *disperse* white light into its constituent colors was first discussed in detail by Isaac Newton. The reason for this dispersion, which is illustrated on page 39, is that refractive index varies with wavelength, being greater for the short wavelengths at the blue end of the spectrum than for the longer wavelengths at the red end. The value quoted for the refractive index of a glass has no precise meaning, therefore, unless the wavelength of the light to which it refers is also given. When a single value is quoted, it is usually n_d, the value measured for the yellow light emitted by helium, whose wavelength is known to be 5876 A, or n_D, the mean value for the double yellow line of sodium, 5893A. Yellow is chosen because it is near the center of the visible spectrum, and the value for such a color is sometimes called the *mean refractive index*.

The difference in refractive index for two arbitrarily chosen wavelengths near the ends of the visible spectrum (red and blue

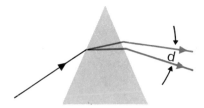

The dispersion of light. Refractive index depends on color, so a glass prism splits a ray of white light into its components. The angle between the extreme rays of the spectrum, d, is the angle of dispersion.

light) is called the *mean dispersion* of the glass. Using n_F, the refractive index for the red line of hydrogen, 6563 A, and n_C, the refractive index for the blue line of hydrogen, 4861 A, to represent the ends of the spectrum, we have:

$$\text{Mean dispersion} = n_F - n_C$$

For a light borosilicate crown glass with n_d given in a glass-maker's catalog as 1.5097, the mean dispersion is 0.0079. A particular double extra-dense flint glass with $n_d = 1.9271$ has a mean dispersion of 0.0441, more than five times as great as the lighter glass. Generally, mean dispersion increases rather quickly as the refractive index goes up, but there is no simple rule relating these two quantities. We shall return to this topic in Chapter 5.

We have said that light can be considered as a form of wave motion. Without going into details, the simplest kind of light wave to picture (though not the most common in nature) is that of *plane-polarized* light, whose waves vibrate in a plane at right angles to the direction of travel, like a string whose particles move up and down when a wave travels along it. Normal glass is "optically inactive," which means that it does not preferentially transmit light with any particular plane of vibration, nor does it rotate this plane. This is what we expect from a liquid, with its random internal structure. However, if the glass is under compression in one direction, the molecules will be pushed together in that direction. A wave traveling with the plane of vibration parallel to the force will see the glass as denser, and so as having a higher refractive index, than a wave whose plane is perpendicular to the force. This is the basis of a method of detecting strains, as shown in the photograph on page 28.

Chemical Stability

There is nothing in the glassy state as such that guarantees chemical stability, and many otherwise potentially useful glasses fail on this account. Soda-silica glass, for example, is quite soluble in water, and this "water glass" has very limited applications. Nonetheless, by proper choice of materials, glasses of very great chemical durability can be prepared. For applications where corrosion resistance, at ordinary or at moderately high temperatures, is required, glass is usually the material of choice.

Pure silica glass is not attacked by water and will resist most acids; the notable exceptions are hydrofluoric acid and, at high temperatures, phosphoric acid. Pure silica is attacked by alkaline solutions, however, and thus common (soda-lime-silica) glasses contain the seeds of their own chemical destruction. When these glasses are exposed to water, the water dissolves sodium ions out of the surface of the glass to form the alkaline sodium hydroxide. This in turn attacks the silica. Newly formed or freshly broken glass surfaces are rapidly attacked in this fashion. Glassworkers put this effect to good use by wetting a glass before scribing it for "cutting." The chemical attack on the surfaces exposed by the scriber initiates regular cracks that assist in getting a clean break.

Common glass exposed to water develops a silica-rich (i.e., sodium-poor) surface layer that protects the glass, or at least slows the attack to where it has no further consequences for most practical purposes. Considerable damage is done, however, and the fragility of common glass is due largely to the numerous minute surface cracks and pits developed by this alkaline corrosion, using the glass's own alkali. We mentioned earlier that newly formed glass will support stresses of as much as 70,000 kg/cm^2, but for practical engineering purposes, a tensile strength of only 350 to 700 kg/cm^2 is assumed. Newly formed glass articles, or those kept in a controlled dry atmosphere, are much stronger than glass that has been exposed to a normal atmosphere, even for a few hours.

Glass "fatigues" under tension—that is, under static load it will ultimately break at stresses lower than those that even aged glass would initially support, and it is the corrosion process just described that is responsible. The initial tension enlarges surface cracks, not enough to start a fracture, but enough to expose new surfaces to chemical attack. As the corrosion proceeds, the cracks open further, and ultimately a crack that was progressing at the rate of fractions of a millimeter per hour by chemical erosion, becomes a mechanical crack spreading at the rate of several thousand meters per second. This fatigue does not develop if the glass is tested in a vacuum or in an inert atmosphere.

For resistance to alkali, the use of boric and aluminum oxides in place of soda and lime is quite successful, and this aluminoborosilicate glass is used in critical applications, such as laboratory and industrial glassware, and for packaging delicate pharmaceuticals. It is fair to say that a special glass can be developed to meet almost any single corrosion problem, but often only by sacrificing other desirable properties. The reverse is also true: Many of the most interesting and sophisticated optical glasses have very poor corrosion resistance, and must be used in sealed cells where they are protected against atmospheric attack. As we should expect, the corrosion resistance of glasses decreases as the temperature rises, and it is particularly important to anneal glass in an atmosphere free from any dangerous contaminants.

Thermal Properties

The linear coefficient of thermal expansion is the fraction of original length at $0°c$ that a material increases per degree centigrade rise in temperature. For glass, values range from 5.5×10^{-7} (5.5 parts per ten million) for pure silica to as much as 125×10^{-7} for certain commercial glasses. The normal range is 60 to 90×10^{-7} for most glass. This is ordinary thermal expansion in the terms of the discussion in Chapter 1. At temperatures over the transformation temperature of glass, the coefficients may increase as much as 50 per cent, because configurational changes as well as normal thermal expansion will occur.

Glass is a poor conductor of heat, and glass exposed to sudden changes in temperature may develop dangerous stresses as a result of temperature difference between the surface and the interior, leading to fracture. For fairly obvious reasons, sudden heating, which puts the glass surface in compression, is less dangerous than sudden cooling, which would put the surface in tension. As a rule of thumb, glass bottles, for example, will withstand heating rates twice as great as the safe cooling rates.

For applications where thermal shock is anticipated, toughened glass offers some advantage, since the surface is already under compression. The problem is usually attacked more directly, however, by using glasses with low coefficients of thermal expansion. Pure silica is ordinarily too expensive (because it is so difficult to fabricate), but 96 per cent silica glass has a coefficient of thermal expansion of only 8×10^{-7}, compared to 5.5×10^{-7} for pure silica, but, say, 90×10^{-7} for ordinary glass. For less demanding service, borosilicate glasses with a coefficient of 32×10^{-7} are satisfactory and these are the basis of the well-known Pyrex brand of heat-resistant glassware. Where excellent corrosion resistance is to be combined with thermal shock resistance, aluminoborosilicate glass (42×10^{-7}) is used.

Electrical Properties

The materials that form glass readily are characterized by strong directional interatomic bonds. The outer electrons of the individual atoms are restricted to these bonds, and thus are not free to conduct an electric current, as the bonding electrons in bulk metal do. Glasses, therefore, have very high electrical resistance, and are, for practical purposes, electrical insulators. On the other hand, a glass is a liquid, and common glasses contain metallic ions (Na^+, for example) that, if free to move, can carry a current. Common glass, then, is an insulator only insofar as its viscosity is so high that the metallic ions are bound in place in the glass and not free to move. The result is that the electrical resistance of glass decreases as the viscosity decreases—that is, as the temperature rises. At sufficiently elevated temperatures, a glass may carry an appreciable electrical current.

An immediate consequence of this conductivity of glass at high temperatures is that it is possible to heat glass by passing current through the molten material. Electrical melting of glass-forming materials may be used where the greatest care must be taken to avoid contamination and to control the process closely. The production of high-grade optical glass is a case in point.

The electrical properties of glass are of particular interest, of course, where glass is used in electrical devices that operate at temperatures above room temperature. Electron tubes, where the internal temperature may be several hundred degrees above the ambient temperatures, are an example. We cannot go into all the details that assume importance in this kind of application, but may mention one point that bears on our general remarks about the nature of glass. The electrical conductivity of glass depends, as we have seen, on the movement of metallic ions within the structure of the glass. Clearly, the closeness of this structure depends on the degree to which the configurational shrinkage previously discussed has proceeded. In making "pinches," which are the small bits of glass used to space the wires in an electron tube, the conductivity of the glass, which operates at an elevated temperature, assumes some importance. It is found that this conductivity may be reduced by a factor of three if the pinches are carefully annealed; the closeness of the carefully annealed structure decreases the mobility of the ions.

Glass Types and Compositions

The compositions and important properties of the major types of glasses at present in use are given in the following pages.

Compositions of Different Glass Types

Commercial Glasses

This list gives the approximate compositions and properties of the main types of glass. The percentages by weight of the main ingredients only are given. The detailed properties depend on the exact composition, and may be sensitive to small changes in minor ingredients. The nature of this dependence is rather complicated, and therefore exact compositions of particular glasses, and the types of minor ingredients, are not given here. As one instance, glass with sodium ions in it usually conducts electricity, yet a high-resistance lead glass is made that contains about six per cent of Na_2O. This is possible because the glass also contains potash, and the potassium ions reduce the mobility of the sodium ions. If these two are present in the right proportions, the total alkali mobility is actually less than with either present by itself.

Pure silica glass

SiO_2:99.5%+

Chiefly used for its low thermal expansion and high service temperature, and when very pure, for its transparency to a wide range of wavelengths in the electromagnetic spectrum and to sound waves. It also has good chemical, electrical and dielectric resistance. Its disadvantage is the very high temperature needed for manufacture, although it can also be made by hydrolysis of $SiCl_4$; in either case it is expensive. It is used for lightweight mirrors for satellite borne telescopes, laser beam reflectors, special crucibles for the manufacture of pure single crystals of silica for transistors, and as a molecular sieve that lets hydrogen and helium through.

96 per cent silica glass

SiO_2:96% B_2O_3:3%

Made by forming an article, larger than required size, from a special borosilicate glass, leaching the non-silicate ingredients out with acid, and treating at high temperature to shrink the article and close the pores. Good thermal properties;

service temperature higher, and expansion coefficient lower, than any other glass except pure silica. More expensive than borosilicate glass. Used for missile nose cones, windows of space vehicles, and some laboratory glassware where exceptional heat-resistance is needed.

Soda-lime-silica glass

SiO_2:70% Na_2O:15% CaO:10%

The addition of soda (Na_2O) and sometimes potash (K_2O) to silica lowers the softening point by 800-900°C. Lime (CaO) and sometimes magnesia (MgO) and alumina (Al_2O_3) are added to improve the chemical resistance. Electrical properties can vary quite widely with composition. This is the most common of all glasses, used in huge quantities for plate and sheet (including windows), containers and lamp bulbs. "Crown" glass is of this type, although modern optical crown glass usually contains barium oxide instead of lime.

Lead-alkali-silicate glass

SiO_2:30–70% PbO:18–65% Na_2O and/or K_2O:5–20%

Lead oxide reduces the softening point even more than lime and also increases the refractive index and dispersive power. "Flint" glass for optical purposes and "crystal" glasses for tableware are both lead glasses. They are also used for thermometer tubes, parts of electric lamps and neon-sign tubes. Compositions vary widely; a glass of high electrical resistance contains about 25% PbO and six or seven per cent each of Na_2O and K_2O; for high refractive index the PbO content may be as much as 65%.

Borosilicate glass

SiO_2:60–80% B_2O_3:10–25% Al_2O_3:1–4%

Low thermal expansion, about one third that of soda-lime glass. Can be made with good chemical resistance and high dielectric strength, and is used where combinations of these are needed. Its high softening temperature makes it harder to work than soda-lime or lead glasses. Used for laboratory glassware, industrial piping, high-temperature thermometers, large telescope mirrors, household cooking ware such as "Pyrex", enclosures for very hot lamps and electronic tubes of high wattage.

Aluminosilicate glass

SiO_2:5–60% Al_2O_3:20–40% CaO:5–50% B_2O_3:0–10%

Another low-expansion, chemically resistant glass that has a higher service temperature than borosilicate glass but is correspondingly harder to fabricate. It is used for high-performance military power tubes, traveling wave tubes, and many applications similar to those of borosilicate glass. Aluminosilicate glass without any boron is especially resistant to alkalis. Nearly all laboratory glassware is made from borosilicate glass, aluminosilicate glass, or a glass called aluminoborosilicate, which contains roughly equal amounts of Al_2O_3 and B_2O_3. The choice depends on the application; thus aluminosilicate glass is used for high-temperature applications or alkali-resistant glass. Alumino-borosilicate glass is slightly better than borosilicate for chemical resistance but has slightly greater thermal expansion.

46

Optical Glasses

The following list gives the approximate weight-percentage compositions of a few optical glasses. The refractive index n_D and constringence V, defined in Chapter 2, are also given. The V values are in descending order because for a particular type of glass they usually go down as n_D goes up.

Light barium crown glass $n_D = 1.54–1.55$ $V = 63–59$
SiO_2:45–50% B_2O_3:3–5% Na_2O:1% K_2O:7% BaO:20–30% ZnO:10–15% PbO:0–5%

Dense barium crown glass $n_D = 1.58–1.66$ $V = 60–50$
SiO_2:30–40% B_2O_3:10–15% BaO:10–15% ZnO:0–10% Al_2O_3:0–10%

Very light flint glass $n_D = 1.54–1.55$ $V = 47–45$
SiO_2:60% Na_2O:5% K_2O:8% PbO:27%

Very dense flint glass $n_D = 1.6–1.9$ $V = 34–20$
SiO_2:20–40% K_2O:0–10% PbO:50–80%

Special Glasses

The approximate weight-percentage compositions of some less common inorganic glasses are given. Some have been developed for special applications, others are of interest because of their unusual ingredients.

Silicon-free glass for sodium vapor discharge lamps
B_2O_3:36% Al_2O_3:27% BaO:27% MgO:10%

Phosphate glass with high resistance to HF
P_2O_5:72% Al_2O_3:18% ZnO:10%

"Soft-solder" glass with transformation temperature below 400°C
SiO_2:5% B_2O_3:15% PbO:64% ZnO:16%

'Lindemann" glass with low X-ray absorption. All metal atoms have low atomic number
B_2O_3:83% BeO:2% Li_2O:15%

Neutron-absorbing glass with high cadmium content
SiO_2:26% Al_2O_3:2% CdO:64% CaF_2:8%

High-lead-content glass for absorbing gamma-rays or X-rays; also a very dense flint glass
SiO_2:20% PbO:80%

Tellurite glass of very high refractive index (about 2.2) and dielectric constant (static value about 25)

TeO_2:80% PbO:14% BaO:6%

Optical glass with high refraction and low dispersion. n_D=1.68 V=58

La_2O_3:20% B_2O_3:40% Tm_2O_3:20% BaO:20%

Semiconducting vanadate glass

V_2O_5:85% P_2O_5:10% BaO:5%

Semiconducting chalcogenide glass transparent to infrared

As:44% Te:24% I:32%

Two dielectric chalcogenide glasses transparent to infrared

(1) As_2S_3:100% (2) As:40% Tl:20% S:40%

Elemental glass (consisting of a pure element)

S:100%

Photosensitive gold ruby glass

SiO_2:72% Na_2O:17% CaO:11% Au:0.02% Se:0.04%

Photochromic glass

SiO_2:60% Na_2O:10% Al_2O_3:10% B_2O_3:20% Ag:0.6% Cl:0.3% I:0.9%

3 The History of Glass

It is not the purpose of this chapter to present a comprehensive history of glass and glassmaking, but to give a short account of the subject in order to show how the early glassmakers met and solved, or failed to solve, their problems. As we shall see, the basic techniques for working glass are extremely old, and many modern techniques and processes are simply refinements and mechanizations of these old techniques. Except insofar as it affects the history of glass as a whole, the making of optical glass has been excluded from this short history and will be covered in Chapter 5.

For reasons that will be clear from Chapter 1, very little glass as such is found in nature. Where molten rock has been rapidly cooled, however, as for example in the neighborhood of volcanoes, natural glass does occur, though very rarely of sufficient purity to be transparent. The primitive people fortunate enough to live near supplies of this natural glass valued it highly, because, being easily broken into sharp elongated pieces, it could be used

Detail from a French church window dated about 1200. The basic primary colors were obtained by dissolving metallic oxides in the melt; details of features, clothing, and so on were painted on with black or gray pigment that was then fired onto the glass.

Arrowheads made out of glass. Left: an ancient arrowhead from Mexico made of natural glass. Right: one made of bottle glass by an Australian aborigine in the 19th century.

for making arrowheads, knife blades, and other tools and ornaments. Objects made from this hard glossy material have been found all over the world, from Greece to Patagonia. More recently it has been reported that aboriginal tribesmen in Africa and Australia were not slow to find similar uses for man-made glass bottles and even glass insulators taken from isolated telephone and telegraph lines. Examples of arrowheads made by primitive peoples from both natural and man-made glass are illustrated on this page.

Ancient Egyptian and Roman Glass

The earliest examples of man-made glass have been found among the remains of the ancient Middle Eastern civilizations. Possibly the earliest objects made entirely of glass are Egyptian beads dating from about 2500 B.C. Other evidence suggests that glass may have been made by the Egyptians as long ago as 3000 B.C. or even earlier than this. At Ur in Mesopotamia, glass beads believed to be nearly 4500 years old have been unearthed. Most of these early examples are small and use glass simply as a bulk material; there seems to have been no early appreciation of the ways in which glass can be manipulated when it is hot and plastic. Some small glass vessels, believed to be of Mesopotamian origin and nearly 4000 years old, were actually carved laboriously from solid blocks of the material.

Many of the earliest examples of glassmaking simply use the

material as a decorative glaze for pottery and stone. The earliest glass vessels, made in Egypt during the 18th Dynasty (1500–1350 B.C.), were made by a method that was in essence an extension of the glazing process. A core or former of sand was given a number of coatings of molten glass: When the coatings were thick enough to be self-supporting, the glass was cooled and the sand core removed. Threads of soft colored glass were then pressed into the reheated article as decoration.

Glassmaking techniques spread gradually from Egypt to neighboring countries and by the sixth century B.C. reached most parts of the eastern Mediterranean. During the Ptolemaic period (323–30 B.C.) glassmakers in Alexandria perfected the making of composite colored glass canes or rods. Made by drawing together a number of glasses of different colors, these mosaic rods, as they are called, can be cut into slices to reveal a repetitive design. Dishes and bowls made by fusing together these slices on a simple sand-core mold were made by Egyptian and later Roman craftsmen. Glass-mosaic panels were also used to decorate furniture and interior walls. The Portland Vase, made by Roman craftsmen in the first century B.C. or A.D., is perhaps the best-known example of another process originally developed and perfected by the glassmakers of Alexandria. This glass-cameo technique consists of coating a glass vessel (in the case of the Portland Vase, a blown vessel) with a layer of glass of a contrasting color that, when cooled, is partly cut away to produce a relief design against a contrasting background.

The first important revolution in glassmaking technique was the invention of the *blowing iron*. Probably first used in Babylon in about 200 B.C. and later in Egypt, this was an invention equal in importance to that of the potter's wheel. Consisting, as it does today, of a hollow iron tube 100–150 cm. long with a knob at one end and a mouthpiece at the other, it enables the glassworker to shape, by blowing at one end, a blob of hot glass adhering to the other end. We know neither the name of the inventor of this simple but revolutionary device, nor the precise date at which it was introduced, and this is typical of the gaps in the history of glass. The *pontil* (or *punty*), a solid iron rod on which hot glass can be taken up and shaped by spinning, squeezing, swinging,

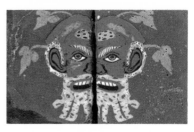

Above: Egyptian sand-core jars, made by building up layers of molten glass on a core of clay or sand that was afterwards removed.

Right, top and center: Glass-mosaic bars like this were made by bundling together rods of colored glass that were then fused and drawn into a long cane in which the built-in pattern ran from end to end. The cane was then cut crosswise into thin slices used as inlays for furniture and jewelry.

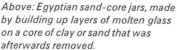

Right: Slices cut from glass-mosaic bars were placed in a mold and fused together to form bowls and dishes such as this Roman millefiori bowl, probably made in the first century B.C.

and cutting, and the *marver*, a slab of polished iron on which molten glass is rolled (marvered) when first gathered on the blowing iron, have similarly vague histories.

The invention of the blowing iron, which is known to have been in use among the Romans during the reign of the Emperor Augustus (27 B.C.–A.D. 14), and the settled conditions of the Roman Empire led to the increase and spread of glassmaking activity. The industry flourished and glassworks were set up throughout the Empire, from Syria to Brittany. Roman glassworkers seem to have mastered almost all the major technical processes involved in glassmaking and decorating: offhand blowing, molding, manipulation with tongs, cutting and engraving, painting, and gilding. Glass objects discovered in Roman Egypt include plates, bowls, goblets, bottles, rings, and even fragments of window glass, and suggest a high degree of technical skill.

Left: The Portland Vase, made by Roman glassmakers in the first century B.C. or A.D., is an example of the glass-cameo technique. The vase, blown in deep blue glass, was given a coating of opaque white glass, which was then partly cut away to leave the raised white figures in relief.

The basic methods of shaping glass are extremely simple. It can be cast, either flat or into a mold of the required shape. It can be molded by pressure, when hot and of sufficiently low viscosity to be forced into the recesses of the mold. It can be shaped by the pressure of air inside it, either offhand (that is to say, freely) or into a cavity mold that will determine the external shape of the expanded article. While still hot it can be bent, twisted, or stretched in tubular sections that retain their cylindrical character in spite of greatly increased length and greatly reduced wall thickness. At higher temperatures, the lower viscosity makes the welding of glass to glass an easy matter. It is this plastic character of heat-softened glass, fully understood and made use of by the Roman glassmakers, that today makes possible the great variety of complex glass laboratory equipment, and thin-walled containers such as electric light bulbs.

The examples of Egyptian and Roman glass illustrated on these pages suggest that early glassmakers applied a great deal of empirical knowledge to coloring their glasses. They knew that specific colors could be achieved by adding particular metallic oxides to the raw materials. Copper was used to give ruby red or green; cobalt, deep blue; manganese, amethyst or purple; antimony, yellow; iron, green, brown, or black; and tin to give an opaque white. Even very small increases in oxide content can produce a great increase in the depth of color obtained, and may sometimes completely change its character. Yet the consistency with which both strong and delicate colors were produced at will suggests a high degree of understanding of the process.

The Middle Ages

The collapse of the Roman Empire brought about a decline in the glass industry. Glass was still produced, but for about a thousand years, from A.D. 200–1200, glass produced in western Europe was much inferior to the achievements of Egypt and Rome. The material itself was poor in comparison, being flawed with streaks and bubbles; the colors were no longer rich, and the range of articles produced extremely small. Only in the eastern Mediterranean, where first the Byzantine and later the Islamic empire carried on and developed distinctive styles, especially in the painting and gilding of glass, did anything like the Romans' technical skill survive. It was in the application of window glass and the skillful use made of stained glass for this purpose, however, that the glassmakers of the Middle Ages achieved their greatest triumphs.

Flat glass, though apparently simple to make, is one of the most difficult forms of glass to produce on a large scale and of high quality. Glass that was clearly meant to be as flat as possible was made in Roman times and even earlier. It was of the type that we should now call cast plate, about a centimeter in thickness, but its finish was so poor and irregular that windows made out of it could have provided only meager illumination and worse visibility. The idea of using colored glass to make decorative windows seems to have originated in Constantinople, where in the sixth century A.D. the Emperor Justinian employed glassworkers to make stained-glass windows in the great church of St. Sophia. Between A.D. 600 and 900 the fashion and the technical skills spread throughout Christian Europe. The earliest examples are simply mosaics of colored glass assembled in a metal framework, but the windows became larger and the figures came to be more subtle as the glaziers grew more skillful, until the final flowering of the 13th and 14th centuries. Hundreds of examples of this particular skill have survived even in European cities whose histories have been largely of recurrent violence.

Not all the stained glass used in the windows of churches and cathedrals owes its color simply to the inclusion of metallic oxides in the melt. In the 13th century a stain made of silver chloride was first applied to the surface of clear glass to produce a golden yellow, or to blue glass to produce a bright green, making it possible to obtain two colors in the same piece of glass. In much the same way a more translucent red than was possible by using copper oxide was obtained by fusing a thin film of such glass onto a sheet of clear glass. Red glass, too, was painted over with the silver chloride stain to produce orange. Methods such as these led to the wider, more subtle color range of most 14th-century stained glass. Later the technique of overpainting broad areas of the finished glass with translucent pigment became widespread, but the finest color effects are those achieved by the colloidal suspension or complete intersolution of the coloring agent in the melt. It seems likely that the composition of stained glasses was often the subject of craft secrecy, since not all makers were able to achieve the richness and purity of the best specimens such as those in the cathedrals of Chartres and Canterbury. To digress for a moment, it seems that, as a general rule, early glassmakers found absolute clarity harder to obtain than satisfactory and closely controlled coloring. Just how hard they found it can be judged from the fact that, until well into the 19th century, the crown glass components of high-quality telescope lenses were almost invariably tinged with green due to the inevitable inclusion of small percentages of iron oxide in their composition. It was the especially high iron oxide content that in the 18th and 19th centuries gave to London bottle glass its

This oil cruet was made in Venice during the 16th or 17th century. Its delicate blown shape, opaque stripes, elegant handle of drawn cane, and the delicate coloring of the rim are typical of the Venetian glassworkers' skill.

characteristic dark green and brown coloring. Venetian and other later glassmakers were to make use of "decolorizers" such as manganese when these tints were undesirable. But a decolorizer is simply a second coloring agent, producing a color complementary to an undesired color, and so rendering the color unnoticeable. The purple produced by manganese dioxide, for example, optically cancels the green of iron oxide. The overall effect is to reduce still further the transparency of the glass. Such a process is useless when maximum light transmission is necessary, but if the original green tinge is slight, the further light loss caused by the decolorizer is likely to pass unnoticed in thin window glass. Carried to extremes (that is to say, a deep green tinge with a decolorizer sufficient to counter it) the method would result in the glass acting as a fairly dense neutral filter.

Many of the techniques used and perfected by the Romans were carried on in the Eastern Empire, though as in Europe the workmanship was less skillful and the material itself poor in quality. With the rise and spread of Islam in about A.D. 1000, Egypt, and in particular Alexandria, became once more the center of world glassmaking. Other centers grew up, such as Aleppo and Damascus, and glassmaking spread throughout the Islamic Empire during the following centuries. The enameling of glass was the most favored form of decoration, and though the glass itself was often far from transparent, the application of arabesque-entwined inscriptions is often extremely effective, particularly in the decoration of the lamps used for lighting mosques. Some objects were actually painted with gold and a metal point used to scratch out the design. From a peak of excellence at the beginning of the 14th century, however, this Middle Eastern tradition of gilt and enameled glass declined, and by the end of the following century it had died out almost completely.

Venice and the European Revival

It was almost certainly the cross-fertilizing influence of the early Crusades that gave fresh impetus to European glassmaking after its relative lapse over a thousand years; and it was Venice that, in about 1200, became the great center of European glassmaking. Secrets and skills were jealously guarded. The compositions and manipulative techniques learned and passed on from generation to generation were regarded as such valuable national property that glassworkers were forbidden to take their skills abroad. A powerful guild was set up in 1279, and in 1291 the mile-long glassworks was moved to the nearby island of Murano, partly to avoid the danger of fire, but chiefly to prevent the escape of valuable experts. The Venetian monopoly, however, was gradually eroded. Rival glassworks were set up in Bologna, Ferrara, and Altare near Genoa, and by 1600 Venetian techniques had spread to almost every country of Europe.

All the lost Roman skills were rediscovered by the Venetians.

Stages in making an air-twist stem for a goblet. First, grooves are made in the sides of a stumpy cylinder of pliable glass; these are then covered over, and the cylinder stretched and at the same time twisted to the required length and pattern. Twists of colored glass can be implanted in the same way.

58

A 16th-century glass furnace.
Note the molds (A), blowing irons (B),
and pliers or pucellas (C) for cutting
glass. Workers are swinging a half-
formed vessel to cool it (left), shaping
on a marver (center), and gathering
or reheating glass at one of the glory
holes (right), while in the background
glassblowing is in progress.

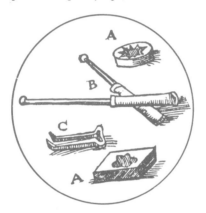

Opaque white glass, made as we have seen by the addition of tin oxide, was placed inside clear glass objects to make delicate strips, spirals, and twists. The ductility of molten glass was for the first time exploited to the full in fantastic decorative embellishments. Plunging heated glass articles into cold water and then reheating produced the fine network of cracks characteristic of "ice" glass. Enameling and gilding were brought to a new excellence. In the 15th century a new clarity and brilliance was given to glass by the use of manganese as a decolorizer, as mentioned above. With an appearance similar to that of rock crystal, this new glass became known as *cristallo* on account of its improved transparency, and quickly became a European fashion.

It seems clear that by the 15th or 16th century great quantities of glass objects were being produced in most European countries, though more is known about what was produced at this time than about the kind of glassworks that produced it. Not only bowls and dishes, but drinking glasses, bottles, and flasks had become relatively common, and houses that did not have at least some glazed windows were becoming increasingly rare. In addition to the evidence of museums, both street names in ancient towns and family names in most European countries still testify to the widespread nature of the industry.

Early glassmaking materials were commonly of the type mentioned in the first chapter: sand, limestone, and soda. "Lime glass" is not only easy to make, but also easy to manipulate, so it is not surprising that it accounted for the bulk of glass production in early times just as it does today. The necessary raw materials may be obtained almost everywhere, and no very sophisticated type of furnace is needed to produce the temperature required for their effective intersolution. The resulting glass has a surface hardness that is satisfactory for a great many purposes; it is chemically very stable and has a usefully low softening temperature that renders it suitable for making objects that may require several resoftenings before completion.

Exact formulas varied from region to region and depended, as they still do, on the availability of different materials. In most of northern Europe, for example, large quantities of soda-ash were assured by the existence of enormous tracts of forest land. Ashes from the burning of hard woods such as oak and beech were especially favored. The Venetian glassmakers, on the other hand, used potash instead of soda-ash for their glass, and this was made by burning seaweed. The silica used almost everywhere was in the form of quarried sand. In most Italian glassworks, however, great use was made of crushed and calcined pebbles that had been selected from riverbeds for their whiteness. The fragments were mixed with broken limestone and the ashes of burned marine vegetation.

Although most industrial units before the Industrial Revolution were small by present-day standards, glassmaking seems to have been an exception. A German writer, Georg Agricola (1490–1555), has described what was probably typical of the most efficient kind of early-16th-century glassmaking plant. He recommends a three-meter-wide furnace, with a length of about 15 meters. The floor, or *siege*, of a glassmaking furnace this size could accommodate a considerable number of large pots of glass.

Such a furnace would have supplied at least several dozen, and perhaps as many as one hundred, glassworkers.

Working procedure seems to have been as follows: Sand, soda-ash, and limestone were well roasted so as to drive out as much moisture and air as possible. Normally the batch was mixed on a hot floor above a subsidiary furnace and, after mixing, was continuously stirred and heated for 24 hours before being used. Then it was shoveled into fireclay pots, which were placed in the furnace ready for melting.

The siege floor, a little above ground level, was roofed over and provided with flues to carry away fumes from the furnace. Fuel was ignited· through a series of holes along the sides of the siege, and the hot gases passed through vents in the floor to circulate within the furnace chamber. Temperature control was obtained simply by confining the vent holes to three, quarters of the furnace's length. Thus one end of the chamber remained at a somewhat lower temperature than the rest, and the pots could, in turn, be pushed into the low temperature region, where their contents would become viscous enough for working.

Tools and organization were no different in broad outline from those that can be seen in a small modern glassworks. The nature of hot glass dictates the methods by which it must be worked, and also, very largely, the organization of the team of workers and the kind of tools that they need. In general, although there was a master craftsman responsible for the main shaping of each work, every article was to some extent a group product.

Among many splendid examples of wineglasses with intricately formed stems, those illustrated here could only have been

A reconstruction of a 16th-century English pot furnace. The model shows clearly the tools used and the pots, both inside and outside the furnace. Wood-fired kilns of this kind were forbidden by law in 1615 in an effort to preserve forests for ship-building, and English glassmakers developed cone-shaped, coal-burning kilns capable of much higher temperatures.

Lavishly decorated 17th-century tableware. Left: blue-tinted wineglass with flowing filigree decorations in clear glass, probably Venetian. Center: covered goblet in the Venetian style with gilded serpentine stem, probably Dutch. Right: engraved goblet made in Nuremberg in 1681.

produced by people who were certain of their skill and their aesthetic judgment. The skills required to produce such high quality tableware are many. The remarkably delicate and regular helixes of the stems involved a number of separate operations. The foot, too, would sometimes be far from simple; its creation called for a number of different actions performed with skill. Rapid spinning of the glass-laden pontil would create a disk of glass that would have to be trimmed to size and properly flattened to provide a reliable base. This might also be decorated with pinched markings, or have small separate pieces of cane or ribbons of glass applied to it or inserted in it by the method illustrated on page 57. Such operations demanded an ability to judge the state of the molten glass almost at a glance, something that could only be acquired as the result of long experience.

Flat Glass up to the 19th Century

Until well into the 19th century by far the most common method of producing window glass in more or less flat sheets depended primarily on blowing. The earliest method, and one still practiced as late as the second decade of the 19th century, initially differed little from that used to produce large flasks or carboys. A sufficiently large gob of glass was taken up on the blowpipe and air was then forced into it to form a roughly spherical globe of 50 or more centimeters in diameter. This globe was then

Six stages in making a simple goblet in the late 18th century. Top row: A gob of molten glass is first marvered to give it a tough outer skin and then blown in a mold to form the cup. After spinning and shaping by rolling the pontil on the arm of the gaffer's chair, the stem is cut and a second bubble of glass attached and (bottom row) flattened to form the base. The goblet is then taken on to a second pontil and the rim cut to shape. Finally, the goblet is fire-finished to remove rough edges (not shown).

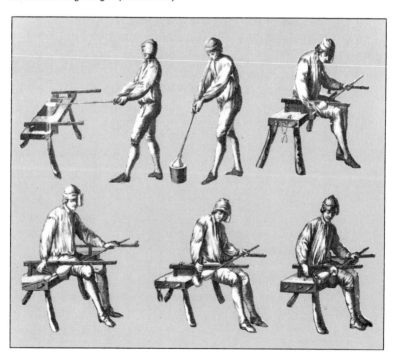

Two stages in the making of crown glass. Left: reheating the open-ended globe on the end of the twirling pontil. Right: Centrifugal force has made the glass flare out into a disk that is then laid down to cool, supported at the rim by a circular ridge of soil to avoid spoiling the fire finish of its surface.

reheated and attached to a pontil, removed from the blowing iron, and marvered so that it resembled a flat-bottomed flask not unlike a modern television picture tube. A circular hole a few centimeters wide was then cut from the flattened base and the glass thoroughly reheated and softened at the glory hole. It was then removed from the heat and the pontil twirled, causing the glass to spin rapidly. Suddenly, under the centrifugal stress created by rapid rotation, the open end of the globe would flare out and the soft glass took the form of a disk. Rotation had to be maintained until the cooling glass was sufficiently rigid to retain its form; but it was never really flat, and its two surfaces were usually far from parallel. Normally the glass was a good deal thicker near the center than at the edge, and the whole surface was marked by a series of concentric circular ridges and hollows. At the very center was a thick blob (the *crown*) revealing the fractured surface where it had been struck from the pontil, and the rings in its vicinity were of a steeper contour than the rest.

Generally disks of up to a meter in diameter were made by this method, but sheets a good deal larger were possible. Because the relative flatness varied greatly from center to edge, only small pieces of reasonable quality could be cut from the sheet, those near the edge being the best. It was this fact, and not any aesthetic preference, that accounted for the small panes and the delicate tracery of dividing bars typical of domestic windows of the 16th and 17th centuries. The thickened and irregular middle section, often dark green, caused a quite remarkable degree of optical distortion, and was fit only for doorways and the upper panes of store windows, or for going back into the melting pot again to make a fresh disk.

The alternative, and more costly, method of manufacturing flat glass was the cast-plate process, first adopted in France in 1688, and later established in England in about 1770. Basically plate glass is cast flat glass, whose surface is poor enough to require, and whose thickness is great enough to allow, further grinding and polishing. In this process molten glass was poured from iron ladles onto an iron casting table, where it was rolled flat by iron rollers. This gave the glass a rough surface that was then laboriously ground and polished by hand. Glass produced by this long and expensive method, being considerably flatter than blown flat glass, was used for windows and, more especially, for mirrors.

Sometimes thick fragments of blown flat glass were put to other uses. The crown, as it was called, was often substantial enough to be used for the fashioning of crude lenses. Occasionally, when the glass was of reasonable homogeneity and had been well annealed, fairly good lenses could be made from this crown glass, and it would be stretching the point only a little to say that this was the humble beginning of the optical glass industry. The term *crown glass* eventually came to be applied to all glass of the type used for windows and bottlemaking. The distinction became necessary because, by the middle of the 17th century, there was a considerable vogue for glass of a quite different formula. This glass, like the earlier Venetian cristallo glass, was called crystal ware because of its especially lustrous quality and its exceptional lack of unwanted color.

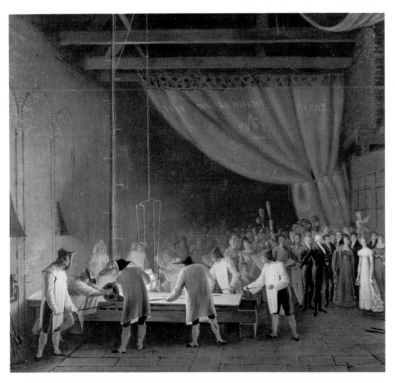

France's great Saint-Gobain glassworks was originally set up by Louis XIV in 1665 to avoid paying Venetian monopoly prices. In this painting, dated about 1820, the Duchesse de Berry watches molten glass being poured out on a casting table to make cast plate.

English Lead-Crystal Glass

The first man to make this new glass was George Ravenscroft (1618–81), an English glassmaker who was researching into ways of improving the luster of his glassware. The first glass he produced was flint glass, made from a mixture of potash, pure sand, calcined flints, and small quantities of niter, tar, and borax. Unfortunately the larger proportion of potash required to counteract the relative infusibility of the flints caused the resulting glass, though attractively clear, to develop a network of minute, but ultimately disastrous, cracks. The addition of lead oxide overcame this weakness, however, and the new lustrous glass proved extremely satisfactory. Lead crystal, also known as *flint glass* (though sand was later substituted for the calcined flints), is heavier and denser than crown glass—that is to say, a prism made from it has greater refracting power than an identically shaped prism made from crown glass. It is also much more dispersive; differently colored light rays emerging from a prism of such material are more widely divergent than they would be after passing through a similar prism of crown glass. Flint glass is softer and more easily abraded than crown glass, and this same softness makes it easy to cut and grind the material to achieve brilliant prismatic effects. In addition the difference in relative dispersion between flint and crown glass led, as we shall see in Chapter 5, to the development of the achromatic lens.

The success of lead-crystal glassware led to an expansion of the British glass industry, hampered only by a steady increase in taxation between 1745 and 1787 to pay for wars against France. As a result many glassmakers moved to Ireland where glass was

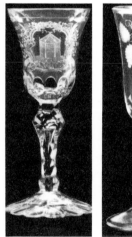

These examples of 18th-century English lead-crystal glass show how this soft, easily abraded material was cut, ground, and engraved to full advantage, in a wide variety of shapes and styles.

Four stages in the evolution of the mold-blown bottle dated, from left to right, c 1650, 1713, 1757 and c 1800. As the process improved, the body of the bottle became narrower and the sides more vertical, until the cylindrical bottle evolved in about 1750. Note the embossed seals bearing the names, initials, or crests of the owners.

duty-free, and important glassworks were set up in Dublin and Waterford.

Nineteenth-Century Glass

The rapid growth of population and pace of urbanization in Europe during the 19th century greatly increased the demand for glass. In America, too, where the first small glassworks was set up at Jamestown, Virginia, as early as 1609, the same expansion took place. Great quantities of sheet glass were needed for windows of all kinds. Glass tableware ceased to be a perquisite of the wealthy. Cheap pressed and molded dishes, pitchers, and flasks began to find their way into households that had previously known only earthen or pewter ware. And the number of commodities packed in glass began to increase rapidly. By the end of the century not only wine, but beer, mineral waters, sauces, pickles, jams, and other preparations previously sold loose, were being sold in glass containers.

Bottlemaking was still a comparatively crude process. The mold-blown bottles of this period were often so grotesquely misshapen that it has been said that before World War I anything could be called a bottle so long as it was made of glass and had one hole in it. There was, however, a gradual improvement throughout the century. In 1821 a Bristol manufacturer patented a method of making bottles in a hand-operated split iron mold that could shape the whole bottle, including the neck; previously only the body of the bottle had been molded. In 1880 another British bottlemaker, William Ashley, invented a semiautomatic bottlemaking machine, and in 1903 an American, Michael Owens, built the first fully automatic machine in Toledo, Ohio.

Sheet glass became flatter with the abandoning of the old crown method. An alternative method of blowing large cylinders that were afterwards reheated, split, opened up, and flattened, though resulting in larger sheets, involved the loss of the natural fire polish on one surface; and flatness was still a very relative term. Ripples and waves were less obvious than in most crown glass, but still gave window glass some very undesirable optical qualities. Toward the end of the 19th century this cylinder method was improved by the introduction of the mechanically drawn cylinder. By lowering a blowpipe with a circular metal bait into the molten glass, raising it slowly, and applying compressed air at fairly low pressure through the blowpipe, it was possible to make a hollow cylinder up to 12 m. long and 75 cm. in diameter.

From the delicate tracery of the ship's rigging to the foamy glass fiber of the sea below, this example of Victorian glass "confectionery" is a triumph of technical skill and ingenuity.

In about 1900 the first step was taken to mechanize the manufacture of flat glass. A circular metal bait was lowered into the melt and a hollow cylinder of glass drawn up and inflated by means of compressed air. After cooling, the ends of the cylinder were cut off, and it was slit open, reheated, and unrolled flat. Cylinders up to 12 m. long and 75 cm. in diameter were made in this way.

The rest of the process was still manual and only one side of the resulting sheet retained the natural fire finish, but the larger cylinder did much to speed up production. The more expensive plate glass was still a comparative rarity until the middle of the 19th century, but quality at its best was very good.

The spate of international exhibitions that began in the middle of the 19th century provided a unique opportunity for European glassmakers to demonstrate their achievement. In Britain, the final removal of excise duties in 1845 led to an enormous expansion in glass manufacture of all kinds, and in time to a more widespread and elaborate domestic use of glassware. This development was reflected by fashion in most European countries, and toward the end of the century glass screens, doors, mirrors, and windows were engraved, sandblasted, and etched with hydrofluoric acid as never before or since. On the dining table of every family with any social pretensions the cut glassware gleamed; candelabra were often positive cascades of faceted flint glass in the form of clusters of prisms of almost every imaginable shape.

Perhaps the most remarkable development during this period, however, was in the field of architecture. The exciting and

The revolutionary Crystal Palace, erected in 1851 in Hyde Park, London, to house the first of the great international exhibitions, was the first large-scale building entirely prefabricated from standardized units of glass and iron. This vast structure had a continuous facade of 80,000 m², contained 300,000 uniform panes of glass, and took only eight months to put up.

revolutionary Crystal Palace, designed and built in London by Sir Joseph Paxton in 1851 to house the first of the great international exhibitions, was the first large-scale building entirely prefabricated from standardized units of iron and glass. Consisting of nearly 300,000 uniform panes of cylinder-blown glass, it was erected in the astonishingly short time of eight months. Most constructions of this kind, however, especially in Paris and London, were utility buildings such as railway stations and market halls, for which there was no traditional style of building. There are many such buildings still standing: The vaulted railway shed at St. Pancras (London) and the market hall near the Madeleine (Paris) are two outstanding examples.

The factories in Europe and the United States that produced this flood of glass products in the second half of the century differed in two important respects from the largest of the 18th-century glasshouses. First, the regenerative furnace, originally developed for metallurgical work, had been adapted for use in melting glass, providing a more efficient use of fuel and a more powerful source of heat. Secondly, the pot furnace had given way to the larger tank furnace, which, as we shall see, lends itself better to continuous production. The story is that in a German glassworks the immense heat of four regenerative furnaces working together cracked all the pots in one of them; molten glass covered the floor of the furnace, but when the pieces of broken pot were removed and more raw materials added, the glass was found to be perfectly good, and the first tank furnace came into being.

Other developments were available to deal with increased demand and to provide the cheap, mass-produced glassware required. A process for pressing glassware mechanically in molds was developed in the United States in about 1827 and quickly taken up in Europe. Bottlemaking, as we have seen, became semiautomatic in 1880 and fully automatic in 1903. Painted decorations were imitated by applying colored transfers. A method was devised of toughening glass (for use in oil and gas lamps) by sudden quenching. By 1900, therefore, a number of developments had come about that were to transform the glass industry in the course of the new century. The regenerative tank furnace, automatic bottlemaking machines, the mechanical drawing of cylinders to make flat glass, the beginnings of the toughening process—all these, together with a growing under-standing of the composition and structure of glass and the incentive to mass production provided by greatly increased demand, were to lead to further mechanization and improvements in the industry, as we shall see in the next chapter.

4 Methods of Production

Glass, unlike metals and most other materials, is usually made into finished products by the producer of the material itself. For example, the whole manufacturing process of a bottle, from furnace, through forming, finishing, and annealing, is almost always completed within the same plant. As a result, glass production lends itself ideally to continuous processes and automation, with all the consequent advantages in efficiency, speed, and economy. In this chapter we shall take a look at the melting process; the different methods of working molten glass, including flat-glass and glass-fiber production methods; finishing and annealing; toughening and laminating; and the decorating processes.

The Melting Process

Great care must be taken in the preparation, measuring, and handling of the raw materials used in glassmaking, since slight variations in the amount of even the minor constituents may have

Newly pressed heat-resistant
ovenware cooling in a block press
mold before further processing.

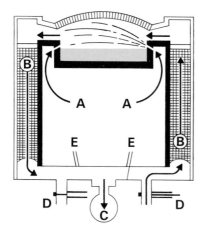

Sectional view of a regenerative continuous glass furnace. Oil-fired burners (A) heat the glass (red). To extract maximum heat from the fuel, hot waste gases from the furnace pass through one of two chambers filled with hollow brickwork (B) on their way to the stack (C). When this brickwork reaches the temperature of the waste gases, valves (D) and dampers (E) reverse the flow so that air preheated by passing through this chamber is used to burn the fuel, while waste gases pass through the second chamber.

profound effects, not only upon the characteristics of the product, but also upon the behavior of the glass during forming, making it either more or less viscous at a given temperature. Since the primary object of glass melting is to convert these raw materials (the *batch* or *frit*) to a homogeneous liquid, uniformity of grain size is equally important; otherwise vibrations during handling may cause smaller grains to find their way to the top of the batch, while large grains are likely to appear as lumps of different viscosity in the final product. In addition to sand, soda-ash, and limestone, which are the basic constituents of soda-lime glass, waste glass of the same type (*cullet*) is also added to the batch, because glass of all types melts at a lower temperature than any of its separate constituents. The addition of cullet therefore speeds up the melting process, and for this reason can constitute as much as 75 per cent of the total batch. The purity of this cullet must be as scrupulously checked as that of the other ingredients. The thoroughly mixed ingredients are spread evenly across the whole width of the furnace.

There are, as we have seen, two distinct types of glass furnace: pot furnaces and tank furnaces. The pot furnace, which today is used only in optical glass making and the crystal-glass industry, normally contains between three and twelve refractory pots, which are slowly preheated in a special furnace (pot arch) to a temperature above 1000°c and are transferred hot to the furnace to avoid the cracking that would occur if they were heated

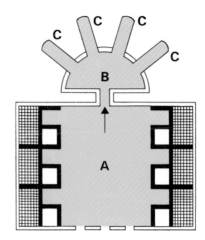

Plan view of regenerative continuous tank furnace. The melting area (A) is divided from the working area (B) by a bridge wall. Molten glass flows, via a narrow throat that prevents the passage of any patches of too high viscosity, to the working area, from which it travels along heated fore-hearths (C) to mechanically operated feeders. These are designed to deliver gobs of the correct size and temperature to the automatic forming machines.

quickly. Most glass furnaces, however, are tank furnaces of the regenerative type.

Molten glass is a highly corrosive substance. One expert has described the process of melting glass as like trying to obtain clear water by applying heat to ice in a container made of sugar. For this reason furnaces, tanks, and glory holes have to be lined with thick walls or refractories especially developed to withstand erosion. These refractories are made of composite clays, usually consisting of several different minerals, both amorphous and crystalline, that deteriorate only gradually under the corrosive attack of molten glass. The gradual erosion of the refractory linings of the furnace is one of the sources of foreign inclusion in glass. Occasionally small fragments are liable to break away from the lining and enter the glass as "stones." Eventually, the furnace lining becomes so deeply scored and pitted by erosion that it has to be renewed. Useful lifetime depends upon the nature of the material used in the lining and the type of glass melted in it. For a tank run continuously the normal life of the lining is between three and four years.

Fuel used in the glass industry depends upon availability and cost. In recent years there has been a gradual conversion from coal—or, to be more precise, producer gas—firing, to oil. This conversion, still far from complete, has been partly the result of relative trends in the prices of coal and oil, and partly due to the easier control and higher melting rates possible with oil.

Mixed and carefully graded raw materials for the continuous production of sheet glass are fed into a hopper from an overhead skip. The raw material (frit) then trickles down at a steady rate to the level of the molten glass in the tank where it is pushed mechanically into the melt that can be seen through the opening in the furnace wall (lower left). The rate of feed is automatically controlled to ensure that the level of the melt is always the same.

Resistance heating is another method used for glass melting that has made rapid strides in recent years. The first stage was the introduction of electric boosting in producer gas or oil-fired furnaces in which molybdenum rod electrodes are inserted through spaces in the refractory walls of the furnace to increase furnace output. Electrodes, suitably placed, not only increase heat input into the glass but also make for easier control of flow currents in the molten glass. More recently, in spite of the high power cost, some all-electric furnaces have come into use. Such furnaces require about 900–1100 kwh to melt one ton of glass, which is considerably more expensive than the one fifth of a ton of fuel oil required to melt the same amount of glass. The advantages of resistance heating over other methods are that furnaces can be smaller and cleaner, cost less to construct, and provide cooler conditions for operators. Higher running costs make this method unsuitable for large-scale glass production, but for special glasses it is a practical proposition.

Severe corrosion in the wall of a furnace. Glass is highly corrosive, so furnaces, tanks, and glory holes are lined with resistant materials. Even so, the life of the lining of a continuous furnace is approximately three years.

A tank furnace may be defined as one whose walls serve both to restrict and retain the heat and to hold the glass. Modern tank furnaces range in size from day tanks in which five to ten tons are melted and refined to be worked into products in one day, to those used in making sheet glass, which can have a capacity of over 1000 tons, and use more than a million m³ of gas per month. Most tank furnaces used today are *continuous*—that is to say, the molten glass is kept at a constant level by feeding the batch at one end at the same rate as molten glass is being drawn off at the other. This type of furnace is, by its very nature, most suitable for high-speed mechanical production. Today, even the optical glass maker uses continuous production for standard melts.

The melting of glass consists of three distinct stages. The first involves the chemical reaction between the ingredients, and results in a sticky mass full of bubbles. The second, or refining, stage consists of raising the temperature to around 1550°c to allow the gases forming the bubbles to come to the surface; it is partly to facilitate this removal of bubbles that chemical agents such as sodium sulfate and arsenous and antimony oxides are included in the batch. At this stage the glass is so thin and watery that it is unworkable. Finally, the glass is cooled until it has the viscosity required for working, generally below 1000°C.

Here it should be stressed that the term "melting" as used in the glass industry can be misleading. Glass is formed by the intersolution of the raw materials. At the usual glass-founding temperature, approximately 1350–1580°C, many of the constituents on their own would still be solid. The melting point of silica, for example, is around 1700°C, while that of calcium carbonate is 2500°C. On the other hand, sodium carbonate and sulfate melt at 850°C and 884°C respectively. The precise manner in which the glass-forming materials react with one another is by no means certain. But it seems likely that some of the reactions that are set in train at a low temperature are necessary preliminaries to the rapid complete fusion at higher temperature. A mixed sodium calcium carbonate forms at about 600°C, and will free carbon dioxide when attacked by the silica. Sodium carbonate attacks silica at 700–900°C and the mixture of sodium carbonate and sodium calcium carbonate melts at 780°C, at which point the reactions are speeded up by the increased chemical activity. Calcium metasilicate will form at 1010°C but such a temperature would be too low to convert all the available material to a molten state quickly enough to be practical. In the continuous process the temperature is so arranged that, as the melting batch begins to form molten glass, it flows down the tank to where the temperature is higher and refining takes place.

Carbon dioxide and other gases liberated from hydrates, nitrates, and sulfates during the melting process, together with air trapped in the interstices of the batch, produce numerous bubbles in the melt. The refining stage, which takes place at a temperature between 1500°C and 1600°C depending upon the glass type, is aimed at complete homogeneity and the removal of all such bubbles, which would otherwise have a weakening effect upon the finished product, quite apart from any optical considerations. Since large bubbles rise more rapidly than small ones, and clear the melt by coalescing with other, smaller bubbles (*seeds*), it is important that the melting process, which produces these gases from the raw materials, should proceed as quickly as possible. If melting is carried out slowly at a moderate temperature, a stage is reached where the large bubbles have escaped, but the melt is full of seeds that rise very slowly, on account of their lesser buoyancy, in spite of the application of higher temperatures at the refining stage.

Finally, the convective flow in the melt assists the molten, refined glass to flow to the forehearth, where, after losing a good deal of heat on the way, the glass is taken off for forming. Before reaching the forehearth the glass passes under a fireclay bridge that acts as a safeguard against possible passage of impurities. Any such impurities are not "scum" in the ordinary sense; in fact they are entirely glassy, but any patches on the surface whose viscosity is too high will be retained by the bridge, which thus ensures a high degree of uniformity in the viscosity of the glass surface in the forehearth.

Glass-Forming Processes

The best known glass-forming process is glassblowing by hand, already described in Chapter 3. The soft lead glasses most suited to this process are cooled to around $1000°c$, at which point they are thick, viscous fluids, orange to yellow in color. The glass to be worked (the *gather*) is taken from a small area on the surface of the melt that has been skimmed and kept clear of surface impurities by a fireclay ring floating on the glass. This method of glass forming has remained practically unchanged since Agricola described it in the first half of the 16th century. It is now used primarily for art glass and fine tableware. Most glass forming of this kind today, however, whether hand or mechanical, is a combination of blowing and molding, and though less spectacular, relies less upon the skill and judgment of the glassmaker, and is faster, more efficient, and economical.

Blowing and Molding

Glass molds are of three types—iron, paste, and press molds— all of which, despite their somewhat misleading names, are usually made of gray cast iron, carefully machined and polished.

Some pressed glass manufacturers, however, prefer steel molds, and during the last few years work has been done with molds made of various alloys such as Incramet, a copper-based alloy. The so-called iron, or hot, mold is in fact a block mold, made in one piece and used for shallow articles that are easy to remove. More complicated is the open-and-shut mold used for large bottles and jars in limited quantities: The mold is filled, an energetic blow of air expands the glass into a thin balloon, the mold is opened, and the jar removed and finished. Two snags limit the use of this method: (1) Heat and the acids in the glass cause the iron to oxidize, crack, and chip away, thus affecting the dimensions of mold and jar; (2) this oxidation affects the

Blowing large flasks in a paste mold. The white-hot gob is cooled to the consistency for blowing (left); the glass is then blown to form a blank or parison (center) that is then blown in the mold, steam preventing contact with the sides. Finally the jar is removed from the opened mold (right).

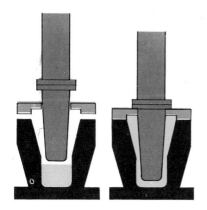

Solid press molding. An air-cooled ring (blue) moves down to seal the space between the water-cooled plunger (gray) and the mold itself (black), forming the upper surface or rim of the article (yellow). Solid molds, having no joints, are inexpensive to make and maintain, and are used to produce articles of simple shape.

surface of the article, making it cloudy so that further polishing is necessary. The smooth, polished surface of an article blown offhand is impossible with this process.

The paste mold is an iron mold that has an inner lining of some heavy viscous liquid that allows the glass to be revolved while it is being blown. Soap or beeswax is used, sprinkled with flour or sawdust, which then bakes into a granular carbon lining. This is kept moist during the process, and the steam produced acts as a cushion between mold and glass. Excess water and steam escape through vents in the mold. The paste-mold process has the important advantage that ware produced in this way has not contacted anything but steam and therefore has a naturally smooth surface. Chemical ware, tumblers, and special electric light bulbs are made by this process.

A press mold normally has three parts: the bottom or mold proper, the plunger, and the ring. The gather is dropped into the open mold, the ring is placed in position, and the plunger presses down into the hot glass, squeezing it from the bottom of the mold up and around the sides. After a few seconds to allow setting, the plunger and ring are removed, and either a valve or the bottom moves against the article to dislodge it. Complicated, recessed shapes require ingenious mold hinging to ensure easy removal of the finished article. To speed the process, the press mold is water- or air-cooled, either externally or by using chambers hollowed out of the plunger. Solid molds, like the one

82

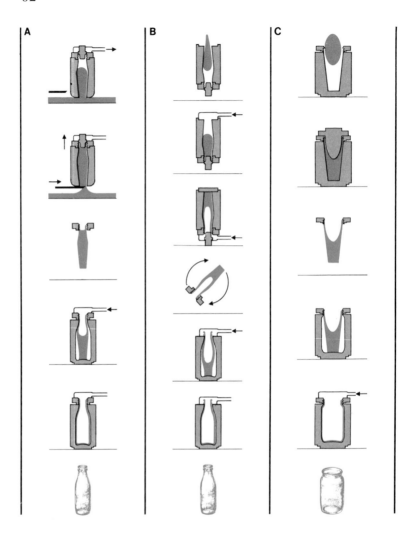

The three principal bottlemaking processes. In the suction process (A) molten glass is first sucked into a blank mold to form a solid blank. In the blow-and-blow process (B) and the press-and-blow process (C) a measured gob of molten glass drops into a blank mold, where it is blown into the shape of a hollow blank (B) or pressed by a plunger (C). In all three processes the blank is transferred to a blow mold for final shaping.

illustrated on page 81, having no joints, are least expensive to produce, easiest to maintain, and produce articles without a vertical seam. Where the shape is asymmetrical, e.g. a jug with a handle, sectional molds are used.

Bottles, jars, and other containers are among the many glass items now produced by complex automatic machines. Molten glass for these machines is produced in a continuous tank furnace. As demonstrated in the diagram opposite, there are three main mechanical methods of bottlemaking, which use two fundamentally different means of providing glass for the bottle: suction and overhead flow feeding. In the first method (A), the mold in which the blank will be formed has the air pumped out of it at one end while molten glass is sucked into it at the other to produce a solid blank smaller than the intended bottle. This solid, cooling blank (called the *parison*) is then placed in a larger blow mold and is blown to the final required shape. In methods B and C the parison is formed by dropping a measured gob of molten glass into a mold where it is roughly shaped by blowing (B) or pressing (C) before being transferred by means of a neck ring to a blow mold for final shaping. The final blowing operation, it will be seen, is basically the same for all three processes shown in the diagram. A complete bottleforming machine consists of anything up to 15 stations, each with its neck ring, blank mold, and blow mold for final shaping.

Temperature control is naturally of the greatest importance throughout the bottleforming process, as in all glass forming, especially during the transfer from one mold to the next. If at any stage the mold becomes too hot the glass will stick and tear inside it, while if it is allowed to cool too quickly proper flow into the final shape will be impossible. For these reasons the working temperature of the bottleforming machine is just as important as the accuracy of the molds themselves, and is kept under constant inspection. Nevertheless, when the shaped bottle finally leaves the machine it is unevenly cooled, the outside having a temperature of around 300°c while the inside is still hot and soft. To avoid the dangerous stresses caused by uneven cooling, the bottle then passes through an annealing kiln, or *lehr*, where it is reheated to about 550°c and cooled slowly. In the case of

Left: a gob of white-hot glass emerging from a mechanically operated feeder just before being cut off. It will then be delivered by the offset chute in the foreground into the mold for pressing. Feeders of this kind deliver from 10 to 40 gobs per minute, each weighing from 100 gms. to 2 kg.

Below: the final stage of the blow-and-blow bottlemaking process. On the left the half-formed red blank is entering the blow mold. In the foreground a completed bottle is being placed on a conveyor belt that will carry it to the annealing lehr.

Right: The neck of a newly blown glass article tapers to a cone. To remove this waste the glass is first scratched with a diamond and then rotated in front of a battery of gas jets so that the intense heat "cracks off" the glass cone and trims the neck of the flask.

Below: Molded ovenware is fire-finished by a number of differently angled gas jets on a 16-station rotating machine. Most molded glass products are given a final polish by applying gas flames to melt away rough edges and mold seams.

containers where the slightest surface irregularity would be a major disadvantage (rims of jars, for instance), a flame is applied to the surface after forming to melt away any machining marks or seams where the edges of the jars meet.

The design and finish of the molds in bottlemaking are of prime importance. Even the blank mold requires precision designing, since the uneven or faulty distribution of glass at this stage will make it impossible to produce a good bottle. Both blank and blow molds must therefore be accurately machined and polished to a near-mirror finish; glassmaking is the only industry in which a mold is required to produce an article to exact dimensions when the temperature of the material is around 1000°c on entering the mold, and when the mold itself is heated to around 500°c. Molds are made of fine-grain cast iron and even the most complex shape can be made accurate to about 0.005 cm. when the mold is new, while those parts of it that form the details of the bottle can be made more accurate still. With working temperatures varying between 450°c and 600°c, the inside surface of the mold slowly wears away through oxidation, and constant attention is needed to maintain its accuracy. The high cost of bottleforming molds (one complete set of molds for producing one type of bottle can involve perhaps 2500 dollars' worth of skilled work) leads manufacturers to adopt ingenious engineering tricks such as spraying molten metal on worn parts or even inserting patches at points of heavy wear. As a general rule a single mold is capable of producing something like a million bottles before it has to be replaced.

Many blown or molded articles require further treatment to remove waste glass, for example, at the mouth of a jar or tumbler. The removal of this unwanted glass is called *cracking off* and the process is now entirely mechanical. First a diamond is applied to the article at the height at which the separation is to be made. The article is then rotated under a battery of hot gas jets. After one or two rotations the intense heat cracks the glass at the scratch, and the upper portion of the article breaks away cleanly. The cut edge is finally fire-polished by passing under another jet of flame that is accurately pinpointed onto the top edge, giving just sufficient heat to melt and round off sharp edges.

Tube Drawing

Most glass tubing is now made mechanically and the hand method, which is slow and wasteful, is only used for small quantities of unusual size or composition. In mechanical tube drawing, molten glass flows from the forehearth onto a hollow, revolving downward-pointing metal core (*mandrel*), giving it a thick, uniform coating of glass. Air flowing through the mandrel at low pressure fills the glass as it is drawn off, forming a tube. Removal is controlled by a drawing device, located 30–60 m. away, consisting of two continuous, asbestos-faced belts that gently grip the tubing, which is by that time almost cold. The tubing is then cut into required lengths. Larger tubing can also be made by drawing the glass vertically from around a circular refractory block immersed in the molten glass; air is blown up through the hollow core of the block to make the tube.

Flat-Glass Manufacture

The methods of making flat glass described in the last chapter have all been superseded, and crown, cylinder-blown, and even cylinder-drawn glass are now only made for special purposes such as when an "antique" appearance is required. In the modern glass industry, four main types of flat glass are manufactured by four distinct processes—flat-drawn sheet, rolled glass, polished plate, and float glass. All four processes are continuous, and, as we shall see, provide the varied types of glass required by today's users.

All the blowing processes of making flat glass were indirect and complicated, and for many years the idea of drawing a flat sheet straight from the tank led to a great deal of experimentation. The greatest difficulty that had to be overcome was in the very nature of molten glass: If a metal bait is submerged in the melt and then drawn up, the glass drawn with it will gradually narrow and "waist" until only a thin thread is left. This and many other problems were gradually overcome and today sheet glass in thicknesses of up to about 2 cm. is produced by a continuous method in which molten glass is drawn, day after day, mile after mile of it, from large continuous tank furnaces. The tank may be as large as 40 m. long and 12 m. wide, and may hold anything

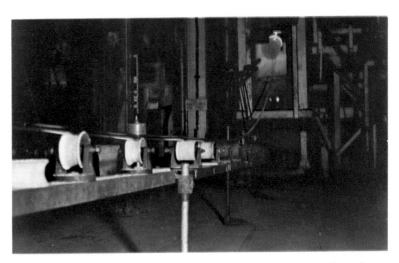

Above: the automatic tube-drawing process. Glass flows down from the tank furnace onto a slowly revolving cylindrical core or mandrel. A steady flow of air is passed through the hollow core, and the tubing, which is kept viscous in the early stages of the process by gas jets, is drawn off continuously.

The flat-drawn glass process. Frit is fed into the furnace at one end (A) at a rate controlled by withdrawal from the drawing kiln (C) where the glass has cooled from the 1550°C reached at point B to about 1000°C. The rapidly solidifying sheet, gripped at the edge by knurled rollers, rises through a vertical annealing lehr (D) to the cutting loft (E) shown opposite.

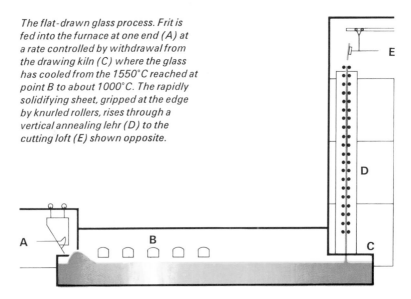

The final stage of the flat-drawn process. An automatic cutter sweeps across the rising glass, and the cutoff piece is removed with hydraulic suckers.

up to 1200 tons of glass in the form of melting frit at one end and homogeneous workable glass at the other. The glass to be worked first passes into a small extension of the tank called the *drawing kiln*, of which there may be as many as four or five to a tank. A bait in the form of an iron grille is lowered into the melt in the drawing kiln and, when the glass adheres to it, the bait is slowly raised, drawing with it a continuous sheet of glass. The rising sheet is gripped by the first of a series of asbestos-covered electrically driven rollers mounted in pairs and enclosed in a vertical annealing lehr. The process having been started, the bait is then cracked off and plays no further part in the operation. The width of the rising ribbon is maintained, and the glass prevented from waisting, in two ways: Firstly, a steel plate called the form, which has a machined slot in it, is placed just above the level of the molten glass and the sheet is actually drawn up through and shaped by the slot; secondly, a pair of knurled, air-cooled rollers grip the sheet at the edges, cooling the glass, and ensuring that the sheet remains constant in width even while its viscosity is low. Without these devices, the ribbon of glass, like treacle from a knife blade, would quickly contract in width, narrow, and become useless. Also facing the sheet just as it leaves the tank are water-cooled steel boxes that serve as heat sinks and thus helps to solidify the sheet quickly. Once the bait has been cracked off, the machine takes over, the whole process becomes automatic, and the flow of the sheet is interrupted only when major repairs are needed. Temperature control at every point is automatic, feed of raw materials is related to withdrawal of the sheet, and not until the rising sheet has hardened and annealed and finally arrives in the cutting loft, 10 m. above the tank, is any manual handling involved.

In the cutting loft, the continuous ribbon of glass is cut to standard lengths and the edges spoiled by the knurled rollers are cut off. The remaining surface has a perfect fire finish. Flat glass produced in this way, however, is never completely free from distortion because differences in composition and cooling rates cause slight differing in thickness and prevent the two surfaces of the sheet from being truly parallel. For this reason it is used where through vision is required but a small amount of distortion is acceptable, for example, in windows for the majority of domestic buildings, in factories, and for greenhouses. For greater freedom from distortion, the more expensive polished or float glass is used.

Probably the simplest and most obvious method of making flat glass is to cast and roll it. In casting, which as we have seen was first used in France in the 17th century, the molten glass was poured onto a large tray-like table, not unlike a large billiard table, made of copper or cast iron, supported by solid masonry. It was then rolled out into a sheet, the thickness being determined by raised metal strips running down both sides of the table, which kept the roller at the required height. From this method has evolved the continuous method of casting in which a ribbon of glass passes through rollers from the working end of a continuous tank and travels horizontally on more rollers into an annealing lehr, at the end of which it is checked and cut into required lengths. Glass produced in this way, however, has come into contact with metal surfaces during its production, which spoil its finish. This method, therefore, is used for making glass for the windows of factories and warehouses where clear vision is not a primary consideration, and also for making wired and figured glass. This last is given its pattern or texture, usually on one side only, by means of a patterned roller, as seen in the illustration on page 92.

Flat glass produced by the casting process, though generally flatter than sheets produced by the crown and cylinder methods, always has one important disadvantage. Its surfaces are spoiled by coming into contact with metal table and rollers. These rough surfaces require further grinding and polishing to give them the clear, undistorted vision or reflection necessary for windows and mirrors. These additional processes, originally done by hand, naturally increased the cost of *polished plate*, as it was called, and as early as 1789 steam was introduced as the motive power for grinding and polishing in an attempt to speed up the process and cut down cost. As larger plates were produced, the methods of grinding and polishing kept pace with progress, and metal disks or tables up to 12 m. in diameter were used. The glass was placed on the disks in a bed of plaster of paris, and the glass polished, turned, and then polished on the other side. In 1921 a great advance was made with the introduction of the Bicheroux process. In this, the glass, though still melted in clay pots as before, was rolled into a sheet between rollers instead of being poured onto a casting table, resulting in a flatter sheet and thus cutting down the time and cost involved in the subsequent grinding and polishing stages. Continuous grinding and polishing machines, first developed in 1927, applied the same principles as described, but the process was still cumbersome and expensive.

In 1937 Pilkingtons of Great Britain evolved the twin grinder, which was capable of dealing with both sides of the plate simultaneously. Today a continuous ribbon up to 250 cm. wide leaves the glassmaking tank between rollers and passes, without interruption, into a machine in which it travels between grinding heads at about 500 cm. per minute. This technique replaced all previous methods of grinding and polishing plate glass, achieved a closer approach to perfect flatness than ever before, and did

The continuous-casting process. Molten glass from the forehearth passes between a pair of casting rollers. The red-hot, semitransparent ribbon then moves on more rollers to the annealing lehr. Rough-cast, figured, and wired glass are among the types of flat glass made by this process.

much to make the production of glass of this kind more economical. Glassmakers, however, still continued to examine the possibilities of discovering a process that would combine the fire-finish of sheet glass with the flatness attainable by the continuous plate process.

The basic requirement for producing a flat, fire-finished, distortion-free glass was some means of preventing contact between anything solid and the glass in the molten or plastic state, at the same time avoiding mechanical stress on the glass. Pilkingtons again were the first to apply the idea of floating the molten glass on the smooth surface of a molten metal at a strictly controlled temperature, and in an inert atmosphere to prevent oxidation of the metal. Tin was found to be the most suitable metal for this purpose, and in 1959, after seven years of intensive and highly secret development work, the first glass was produced commercially by the revolutionary float process.

In the float process, the frit is fed into the filling end of a continuous glass tank and is melted in an oil-fired regenerative furnace. The molten glass leaves the furnace in a continuous strip and floats straight onto the surface of an enclosed pool of molten tin. Throughout this crucial stage the glass is surrounded by a controlled atmosphere and heated sufficiently for all irregularities on both sides to flow out and for both surfaces to become flat and parallel. As the continuous ribbon passes along the length of the bath it is gradually cooled sufficiently to prevent damage to the surface when it leaves the float bath chamber and moves into the annealing lehr. Although simple in principle, the whole success of this process depends upon a precise balance between hot glass, hot metal, and hot atmosphere. Glass produced in this

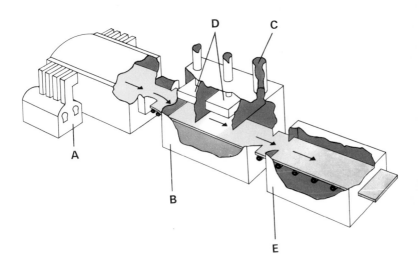

The float-glass process. Molten glass emerges from the furnace (A) into the float bath (B) where it literally floats on molten tin (red) in an atmosphere that is carefully controlled (C) to prevent oxidation of the metal. Heat applied from above (D) melts out any irregularities, so the glass is free to conform to the flat surface of the tin. The glass is then cooled sufficiently to be fed onto the rollers in the annealing lehr (E) without spoiling the underside finish.

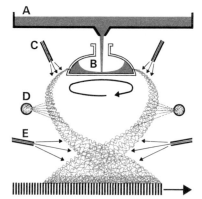

In the crown process of glass-fiber manufacture, molten glass falls from the forehearth (A) into a rapidly rotating dish (B) with hundreds of small vents around the periphery. Glass is thrown out to form fibers that are first controlled by blowing rings (C), then, after being sprayed with a suitable binder (D), are again blown (E) to ensure random distribution as wool on the conveyor belt below.

way is exceptionally free from distortion and the fire-polished surfaces are brighter and better than those achieved by the expensive grinding and polishing processes. Originally manufactured in the most widely used thickness, $\frac{1}{4}$ in. (0.64 cm.), float glass can today be made at half this thickness as the result of further improvements in technique. Glass of this kind is now being made commercially not only in Britain, but in the United States, France, Russia, Japan, and elsewhere.

Glass Fiber Manufacture

Glass fibers are by no means a recent discovery—in the 13th century the Venetians used finely drawn glass, as we have seen, in the intricate decoration of their glassware. Modern technical development, however, dates from World War I when Germany was cut off from supplies of asbestos, and a substitute insulating material had to be found. Today glass fiber consists of two main kinds: glass wool and continuous filament.

Until recently several methods were used for making glass wool, but now production is almost entirely by means of the crown process, which is the result of development work carried out in France and the United States. A fairly thick stream of molten glass is allowed to fall from the forehearth into a rapidly rotating steel alloy dish that has many hundreds of tiny vents around its periphery. Glass is then thrown out through these apertures by centrifugal force, forming fibers that are first

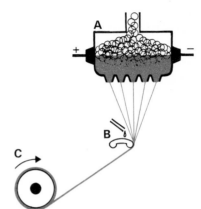

In the marble bushing process for making continuous filament yarn, filaments are drawn direct from an electrically heated bushing (A) into which previously made glass is fed in the form of marbles. These filaments are collected and size is applied to keep them together (B). The combined single strand is then wound on a high-speed winder (C). The continuous yarn is made up of between 100 and 400 individual fibers.

controlled by blowing rings and, after spraying with a suitable binder, are given further air treatment to ensure random fiber distribution in the resulting mat. A conveyor belt then carries the fiber away, first to curing ovens and then to trimmers and guillotines that shape the final product, normally into either flexible mat or rigid board. Very fine textures are obtainable, with individual fibers of a diameter of approximately 0.0007 cm. A small amount of lubricant is sprayed on the fibers to prevent their being injured by friction, and the final density of this matting varies between 80 and 130 kg/m³.

The aim of the continuous filament process is to produce a continuous strand consisting of up to about 400 individual glass filaments, and two principal methods are now in use. In the more common direct-melt tank method, molten glass passes from the furnace through the forehearth to a series of bushings containing the required number of accurately dimensioned forming tips. Fine filaments of glass are drawn down on rollers from the bushing tips at a speed of several thousand meters per minute; each of these filaments may be as fine as one tenth of the diameter of a human hair, and visible only when light catches it at a certain angle. The filaments are then gathered up, sizing is applied to keep them together, and they are combined into a single strand on a high-speed winder.

In the older marble bushing method, the yarn is made by drawing filaments directly from an electrically heated bushing

Bottles entering and leaving the annealing lehr. After forming, glass products are cooled to about 300°C and reheated to about 550°C to remove stresses. They are then cooled slowly to prevent further stresses occurring.

in which glass, already made and formed into "marbles," has been remelted. The glass is fed into the bushing in the form of marbles because this minimizes the danger of uneven viscosity due to the introduction of cooler raw materials to the melt. Uniform viscosity and therefore even flow through the bushing nozzles is naturally of the highest importance in drawing very fine continuous filaments in this way.

Annealing

As we saw in Chapters 1 and 2, the shrinkage of glass on cooling is a complex phenomenon. At temperatures above the transformation temperature, glass shrinks on cooling by ordinary thermal contraction and also by a configurational shrinkage whereby the glass comes to a more dense, or less open, internal structure. Below this transformation temperature, only normal thermal contraction occurs. However, the transformation temperature at which the configurational shrinkage ceases is determined partly by the cooling rate; the more rapidly the glass is cooled, the higher the temperature at which this configurational shrinkage ceases. See, for example, the diagram on page 26.

Glass is a poor conductor of heat, and in shaping glass it is inevitable that some parts of a piece will cool more rapidly than others. Accordingly, the configurational shrinkage will be arrested sooner in these more rapidly cooled parts. The effect will initially be offset by the temporarily greater normal thermal shrinkage of the rapidly cooled part, but when the entire piece has cooled, there will be a greater total shrinkage (configurational and normal thermal shrinkage combined) in the parts that cooled more slowly. The result is that serious internal stresses may develop, and these will be permanent, unless they are relieved by subsequent treatment. For simple shapes, under carefully controlled conditions, this effect can be exploited to produce toughened glass. The random occurrence of these "frozen-in" stresses produces weakness in most glass products, however, and can even lead to spontaneous fracture when the article is cooled to room temperature. For this reason all commercial glassware, after shaping, must be reheated to a temperature at which these frozen-in stresses can relax by internal flow of the glass. The temperature used is below that at which the articles would seriously deform under their own weight, of course. When the internal stresses have had time to relax, the articles are cooled slowly, and therefore more uniformly, to a temperature well below the transformation temperature, and finally, somewhat more rapidly to room temperature. This is the process known as *annealing*.

Early glassmakers used a haphazard form of annealing that consisted of placing just-finished articles in a chamber above the melting pot. Later this chamber was built as a separate unit or oven in which the day's completed glassware was placed, sealed, heated, and allowed to cool over a period ranging between three days and a week. Better understanding of the theory of annealing, largely the work of Adams and Williamson in the United States at the beginning of this century, enables modern glassmakers to carry out the process just as effectively in a fraction of the time. For example, the region in which the temperature must be lowered most slowly is around the transformation temperature. Once the glass is safely below the temperature at which the configurational shrinkage effectively ceases, there is no further danger of freezing in areas of differing densities that will lead to stresses on further cooling. In the last part of the annealing schedule, the major danger is that of breakage from temporary unequal contraction caused by normal thermal shrinkage. The earlier glassmakers did not understand this process in detail, and one suspects their temperature control was not very precise; in any event, their cooling schedules were very conservative.

Annealing is carried out either (1) in batches, in lehrs that are filled, heated, and cooled (most optical glass is annealed in this way), or more often (2) by passing the glassware by conveyor belt through a tunnel-shaped lehr between 10 m. and 35 m. in length within which a suitable temperature gradient is preserved. Some tunnel lehrs are known as *muffle* lehrs, because the glassware is insulated or muffled, usually with walls of fire-resistant clay, against the flame gases to avoid the discoloration caused by some high-sulfur fuels, while numerous draft and ventilation adjustments provide close control of the annealing temperature. The flames are carried in flues on all four sides of the muffle to distribute the heat as evenly as possible. The actual heating area takes up only a third or a quarter of the total length of the lehr. The conveyor belt is formed of woven wire and passes over rubber-covered rollers. Such lehrs, also called *unit* lehrs, usually each deal with the output of one automatic forming machine. They operate at about 30 cm. per minute and thus complete the annealing process in approximately 1 hour depending upon the thickness of the articles passing through. An innovation among annealing methods that is an indirect result of mass production processes in the glass industry is the so-called *heatless* lehr. This makes use of the fact that glass when first placed in the lehr is still hot from the furnace. With accurate control of the speed of transit through the lehr, and consequently of the annealing temperature, glass articles can themselves provide all the heat necessary for perfect annealing.

Toughened Glass

Legend describes how the Emperor Tiberius, on being shown how the strength of glass could be greatly improved by a quenching or sudden cooling process, ordered the inventor to be put to death at once because he feared that such a priceless material as toughened glass would prove more valuable than all his treasure. Prince Rupert of the Rhine in the 17th century found that a drop of molten glass allowed to fall into water became tear-shaped, and that the head of the drop was strong enough to resist a heavy blow. On fracture, moreover, "Rupert's drops"—as they are called—will disintegrate harmlessly into finely powdered glass. It was not until 1874, however, that a Frenchman named de la Bastie patented a method of toughening flat glass by quenching in oil, and only during the last 50 years or so has air-quenched toughening found widespread application in the glass industry.

The toughening of glass is essentially the opposite of annealing. The article is heated to a temperature above the transformation temperature, and the surface is then rapidly chilled. The surface temperature drops below the transformation temperature more rapidly than the configurational shrinkage can take place, and the less dense structure appropriate to the higher temperature is frozen-in in the surface region. The interior, cooled less rapidly, continues to undergo configurational shrinkage for a longer time, and tries to reach a more dense structure. When the entire piece has cooled the interior will have been prevented from shrinking fully; the interior will then be in tension, the surface in compression.

Ordinarily glass is not strong in tension, but this is only because cracks, spreading from the surface, propagate rapidly across the entire piece. But the interior of a piece of toughened glass, which is the portion in tension, has no "surface" from which cracks may spread. The physical surface of the piece is compressed, as a result of the internal tension, and a crack cannot penetrate unless it overcomes this surface compression. As a result, commercial toughened glass will withstand impacts five times as heavy as those that normally annealed glass of the same composition can stand. This is only another way of saying that the glass must be bent further before it will break; it must be bent sufficiently far that the surface on the exterior of the bend is no longer compressed.

The tensed interior of a piece of toughened glass represents a considerable amount of stored energy, and when a crack does penetrate to the interior, the abrupt release of tension causes shock waves that rapidly shatter the entire piece. The fracture surfaces characteristically meet the glass surface at right angles, and a toughened automobile windshield, on fracturing, disintegrates into a relatively harmless set of cubes, looking much like a pile of coarse rock salt. Thus the toughened glass is not only stronger than normally annealed glass, it is also much less dangerous when it breaks.

All the shaping and cutting of a toughened glass article must be carried out before the glass is toughened. The conditions required for the actual toughening—the temperature of the furnace, the heating time, air pressure, quenching time—must be very accurately controlled. Conditions are adjusted so that when toughened glass is broken under certain standard conditions, there should be at least 60 particles to every six square centimeters. Samples are fractured from time to time to make sure that this standard is maintained. All glass toughened in this way is given one test blow with an automatic wood-faced hammer, resulting in an impact roughly equivalent to a 0.75 kg. steel ball falling from a height of 1.5 m. Finally, the glass is examined in a strain-viewing apparatus to check that the strains created in the glass are uniform.

Laminated Safety Glass

Laminated safety glass is a sandwich consisting of two layers of ordinary annealed glass bonded together with a sheet of transparent material in between. On fracture, this flexible, plastic interlayer holds the fragments of glass together so that the material will crack but hold. Its discovery is usually attributed to Edouard Bénédictus, a French chemist, who in 1903 noted the behavior of a glass flask that he accidentally dropped in his laboratory and that had previously contained collodion, or ether salts: "All the contents had evaporated over 15 years, leaving the interior of the flask covered with an extremely tough layer of celluloid enamel. The splinters held firm in such a way that at the moment of impact not a single one became detached or even seemed likely to do so." It was not until some years later that

Breaking a Rupert's drop. Made simply by dropping molten glass into water, heads of such drops can resist a heavy blow, and demonstrate the principle of toughened glass as described on page 99. The interior region is under great tension, so that when the surface is broken in a single place the whole drop shatters immediately into small fragments.

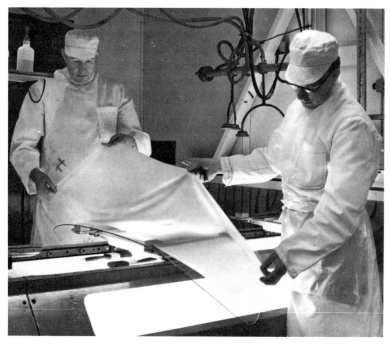

Assembling vinal and glass to make a curved laminated windshield. After preliminary adhesion, the assembled glass sandwich is placed in an autoclave where an air pressure of 7 kg/cm² and a temperature of 100°C complete the lamination process.

Bénédictus saw in this a way of preventing the dangerous shattering of glass, in particular in the case of automobile windshields. Celluloid, originally used for the transparent interlayer, soon proved unsatisfactory because of its tendency to turn brown with age, and today a plastic material called polyvinyl butyral, generally known as *vinal*, is used. In addition to its safety properties, if a thick interlayer of vinal is used, laminated glass can reduce the noise level in a room by as much as 15 decibels below the level that could be achieved with ordinary glass of the same total thickness.

When curved windshields for automobiles are to be made, matched pieces of glass are passed through an electric furnace where they sag together onto a stainless steel frame of the required curvature. The required temperature is, of course, much greater than that at which the vinal interlayer would be destroyed, and the interlayer must therefore be inserted after the curved glass has been cooled and annealed. The interlayer, which is applied in sheet form, is first dried thoroughly to reduce its moisture content to less than half of one per cent and subsequent handling is done in an assembly room that is air-conditioned to a value not exceeding 30 per cent relative humidity. The temperature is kept at 16°C to prevent parts of the interlayer from sticking to each other.

The assembled glass sandwich first passes through a series of electric heaters and rubber rollers to bring about preliminary adhesion, and is then placed in an autoclave. Here air at 7 kg/cm² is admitted and the temperature raised to slightly above 100°C. After application of heat and pressure the transparent vinal interlayer is not much more than 0.4 mm. thick. Subsequent cooling is slow to prevent cracking, but when the shield is removed from the autoclave adhesion is complete and the laminated windshield ready for use.

Decorating Processes

There are a number of ways in which glass products can be decorated after they have been formed and annealed. Intricate designs can be made by removing small amounts of glass by means of etching, sandblasting, or grinding, or considerable quantities by means of cutting. Other methods consist of partly or completely obscuring the glass itself by means of fired enamels or by silvering.

The discovery that hydrofluoric acid would readily attack glass was made in Sweden at the end of the 18th century. The acid combines with the silicates to form soluble fluorides that can easily be washed from the surface. Since a strong acid solution makes the glass surface translucent and roughened, a solution of sulfuric and hydrofluoric acid is generally used to give a smoother, more brilliant surface. A matt surface can be achieved by applying hydrofluoric acid vapor.

In needle etching the glass is given a coating of a resist such as beeswax, paraffin, or rosin and the required pattern is scratched on with a steel needle. The article is then immersed in hydrofluoric acid solution for about ten minutes. Warm water is used to remove both resist and solution. Glass can also be given a white finish by the application of ammonium bifluoride mixtures. In the making of translucent electric light bulbs, for example, the inner surface is first coarsely etched by spraying with a strong ammonium bifluoride solution. This is followed by a spray rinse with a more dilute mixture that smoothes the surface left by the first etching. Ammonium bifluoride is also used in the ink for drawing designs in glass.

Sandblasting is an inexpensive method of making glass translucent by bombarding it, by means of compressed air, with coarse, round-grained sand. Patterns can be achieved by masking parts of the surface with a soft rubber stencil. The effect produced though rougher than that obtained by grinding, is adequate for inexpensive mass-produced glassware.

The lead-crystal glassware intended for cutting is made strong and heavy to allow the deep cuttings that refract light and show up prismatic patterns. The decoration is first inked onto the article as a guide and the design cut by a slowly revolving wheel of sandstone or Carborundum, using water for cooling and for removing waste. There are three basic types of cut: hollow cut, made by a convex wheel; bevel cut, which is V-shaped; and panel cut, which is flat. The rough white surface left by cutting is removed either by hydrofluoric-acid etching or by polishing on felt wheels with a fine abrasive. Copper-wheel engraving, which produces shallower cuts, is more suitable for decorating lighter, thinner glassware. Linseed oil mixed with emery powder or Carborundum is fed onto the revolving copper wheel to provide an abrasive. So precise are the results obtained by this method that to produce a fairly simple design an engraver may use as many as 50 wheels ranging in diameter from 3 mm. to 10 cm.

A wide range of both transparent and opaque colors may be applied to glass surfaces, and when fired in special decorating lehrs they become reasonably permanent. Many of these are applied by painting the article with an organic metallic compound that, after firing, leaves an extremely thin film of the metal on

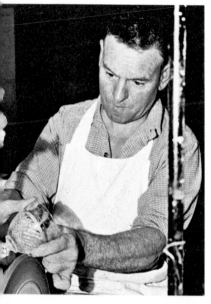

Decorating a cut-glass article by pressing it onto a slowly revolving wheel of sandstone or Carborundum. Water cools both glass and wheel, and removes waste. The roughness of the white surfaces left by the wheel is removed by etching with hydrofluoric acid or by polishing with a felt wheel and a fine abrasive.

Copper-wheel engraving. Linseed oil and emery powder are fed onto the revolving wheel to act as a gentle abrasive. As many as 50 copper wheels, between 3 mm. and 10 cm. in diameter, may be used to engrave a simple design.

This general view of the enclosed bath of molten tin used in the float-glass process, looking back toward the tank furnace, gives some impression of the massiveness of the operation.

the surface of the glass. An alternative method is to apply an inorganic oxide colorant in some organic vehicle that will disappear during firing. A third method is enameling. The enamels used generally consist of low-melting-point glasses. These are applied by sprinkling or dusting them in fine powder form onto a surface that has previously been given a light coating of gum or varnish. Alternatively, the colorant can be mixed with a vehicle such as a volatile oil and applied to the surface of the article by a screen-printing process. Iridescence can be achieved by adding small proportions of silver and bismuth to the batch. The formed glass is then subjected to a carbon-rich flame, which partly reduces the silver, giving an iridescent surface.

Because of the numerous and varied defects to which glass itself is prone, all glass products must be thoroughly inspected after manufacture. Internal faults include "stones" (nonglassy matter embedded in the glass, such as undissolved silica, minute pieces of refractory material from the furnace, or crystals due to devitrification); "cords" (narrow bands of glass with a different index of refraction from the rest due either to local but extreme differences in composition or to uneven cooling during manufacture); and air bubbles, both large (blisters) and small (seeds). Surface irregularities are caused in a number of ways: by bad mold seams, particles of iron oxide from molds, or cracks caused by the glass, when just below softening point, coming into contact with a cold tool or surface. All these possible imperfections, with more fundamental failure to meet dimensional specifications due to bad mold-making or simply mold wear, make it understandable that for most glassware 95 per cent selection is exceptionally good, and selection of around 75 per cent may be considered normal.

In 1900, methods of glass production were not basically very different from those in use 50, 500, or even 1500 years before, in that they were all essentially hand-worked, batch methods. Today, melting, blowing, pressing, drawing, rolling, annealing, in fact every stage of glass manufacture, has become mechanized and continuous. From the Pilkington continuous flat process to the Corning ribbon machine, capable of turning out over 1000 electric light bulbs a minute, mass-production methods have revolutionized the glass industry.

5 Optical Glass

Glass is the most common transparent rigid material, and one of its main uses is for refracting light. Glass used for making lenses and prisms must be extremely uniform in its optical properties, and the components themselves must be made to precise shapes and have surfaces of very high quality. For these reasons special techniques have been evolved that are different from those used in most other parts of the glass industry.

Optical Problems and the Glassmaker

The designer of lens systems must be supplied with glass of uniform and precisely specified refractive index. But there is more to his needs than that, for there are certain optical problems that he can solve only with the cooperation of the glassmaker.

An example is *chromatic aberration*, the fault caused by the phenomenon of dispersion, discussed in Chapter 2. Instead of forming a sharp image, the lens brings each color to a focus at a different place. This is shown in the diagram on page 110.

Polishing a block of lenses. Holes in the polisher let the slurry of water and cerium oxide through. The block is rotating slowly about a vertical axis while the polisher is free to rotate at random on the block.

110

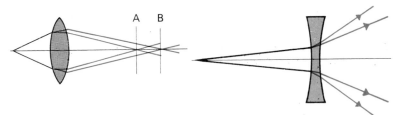

Ideally a lens will bend light so that all rays coming from one point on its axis meet again at a single point, also on the axis. In practice, this is never achieved exactly. One reason is that blue and red light are refracted to different degrees (left); a screen at A would therefore show a sharp image formed by the blue surrounded by a disk of red (and other colors) while at B it would show a sharp red image surrounded by a disk of blue and other colors. The converging lens causes blue light to converge more than red, while the diverging lens (right) produces the opposite effect.

   This diagram also shows the different kinds of dispersion produced by converging and diverging lenses, and it is this difference that makes it possible to cure the aberration. The basic idea is that if we cement a converging lens and a diverging lens together so that the light passes through them both in succession, the dispersion produced by the second can be made to cancel exactly the dispersion produced by the first. However, calculations show that if both lenses are made of the same kind of glass, any combination that causes the dispersions to cancel each other will also make the deviations cancel. Every ray will emerge traveling parallel to its original direction, and the lens will not be capable of focusing light at all. This is where the glassmaker comes in. If we have two different kinds of glass, such as the types known as *crown* and *flint*, we can use them in the way just described to overcome chromatic aberration. The *achromatic doublet*, as the combination is called, is illustrated opposite.
   From this diagram we see that it is important to know the ratio of deviation to dispersion for any type of glass. This will depend on the type and shape of the component, of course, but as a rough measure the quantity called the *constringence* (denoted by V) is used:

$$V = \frac{n_d - 1}{n_F - n_C}$$

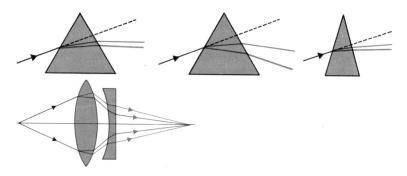

A prism of crown glass (top left) produces deviation and dispersion (see diagrams on pages 37 and 39). A flint prism of the same size produces more deviation and much more dispersion (top center). This illustrates the point that flint glass has not only a greater refractive index and greater mean dispersion than crown glass, but also a greater value of the relative dispersion, i.e. dispersion relative to deviation. The third diagram (top right) shows a flint prism that produces the same dispersion as the crown prism in the first diagram; it has a smaller refracting angle and produces less deviation than the crown prism. The bottom diagram shows how a powerful converging crown lens and a weaker diverging flint lens are used in an achromatic doublet.

The reciprocal of this $(1/V)$ is called the *relative dispersion*, because it represents, roughly, the amount of dispersion relative to the amount of deviation. Values of V from 65 (low dispersion) to 21 (high dispersion) are found in commercial optical glass. The essential requirements for an achromatic doublet are two glasses with very different relative dispersions.

But this is not the end of the problem. The fact is that even if the red and blue images formed by an achromatic doublet coincide with each other, they may still not coincide with the images formed by intermediate colors such as green or yellow. The mean dispersion $(n_F - n_C)$ refers only to two particular colors in the visible spectrum, and two glasses may have the same mean dispersion but different *partial* dispersions. They will then disperse red and blue light equally, but one glass will make the green light emerge closer to the red than the other will. This means that there will be residual chromatic aberration even in an achromatic doublet.

One way of reducing this aberration is to make a triplet using three different types of glass. It is then theoretically possible to bring three colors to a common focus. But the ideal way of obtaining a lens that does not produce any chromatic aberration at all would be for the glassmaker to prepare two glasses with precisely specified partial relative dispersions. This will probably never be achieved exactly, but it is certainly possible to reduce the residual chromatic aberration of a doublet by choosing the glasses carefully.

This example is fairly simple, but actual problems facing manufacturers are often very complicated. There are many aberrations apart from chromatic aberration. It is usually possible to eliminate, or greatly reduce, any one of them, but unfortunately the modification that reduces one is likely to make another much worse, and the extra freedom given by a large variety of glasses is very valuable here.

The History of Optical Glass

Lens-shaped objects from Crete, made of rock crystal, date from between 1600 B.C. and 1200 B.C., but we do not know if they were made as lenses or as ornaments. The Greeks knew of burning glasses, as shown by Aristophanes' comedy *The Clouds*, first performed in 434 B.C. A character proposes to escape a summons for debt by getting the sun, at a distance, to melt the wax in which the summons is inscribed, using "that fine transparent stone with which fires are kindled." However, the first definite mention of a magnifying lens is in the works of the Arab optician, Alhazen (died A.D. 1038), who says that an object placed under a segment of a glass sphere appears enlarged. Magnifying glasses were used for reading in 10th-century China, and spectacles were invented in Italy around 1280. By that time glass had become widely used as the material for lenses, and from the start, the techniques of polishing them were taken over from the much older craft of polishing jewels.

In 1591 a good description of lensmaking appeared in a book by Baptista Porta of Naples. In 1671 Père Chérubin d'Orléans produced a treatise that dealt with telescopes, binoculars, microscopes, and spectacles, and included 82 pages about lensmaking, with descriptions of machines for grinding and polishing the lenses. By the time of Isaac Newton (1642–1727) the art had advanced so far that the deficiencies of optical instruments, especially telescopes, were beginning to be felt acutely. One of these—chromatic aberration—was of particular interest to Newton himself. Unfortunately his experiments led him to a wrong conclusion. It was difficult for anyone then to identify light of a particular color exactly, and the glasses then available did not differ much in relative dispersion. Newton came to believe that all glasses had the same relative dispersion, which would mean that chromatic aberration was an inescapable fault in lenses. Newton was anxious to make a good telescope, and he decided that mirrors, which do not produce chromatic aberration, would make better objectives than lenses, which had been used till then. As a result of his work, refracting telescopes fell almost completely out of favor. In those days there was no good way of laying down a thin reflecting film onto glass, so the objectives of the reflecting telescopes that now became common were made simply of polished metal.

It took a second error to correct Newton's. In about 1730 an English amateur, Chester Moor Hall, argued that the optical system of the eye produced an image without colored fringes, and therefore correction of chromatic aberration could not be theoretically impossible. In fact the eye does produce some chromatic aberration, but only an amount small enough to be tolerated. Hall had the idea of making an achromatic doublet from a converging lens of crown glass, and a diverging lens of the newly developed lead-crystal glass, known to opticians as *flint*. A few years later the method was refined by the optician John Dollond, who seems to have discovered it independently of Hall. Urged by his son, Dollond successfully applied for a patent on the achromatic doublet. He did not enforce the patent, but after his death his son did, with disastrous results to the British optical industry. The Dollonds' doublet was not of good quality, but without competition there was no incentive for them to improve it. One reason for its defects was the glass used, which was simply a by-product of the domestic glass industry. As late as the beginning of the 19th century a British scientist complained that "out of every hundred pounds (45 kg.) of goblet bottoms, carafes, and such-like, it is difficult to find a piece good enough to make a three-inch (7.5 cm.) objective."

The initiative passed to the Continent, where a French-Swiss, Pierre Louis Guinand, used new methods of stirring to produce homogeneous flint glass. Flint glass contains lead oxide, which is very dense and normally sinks to the bottom of the melt. Guinand achieved his success by cooling the melt very slowly and stirring it the whole time. For a while, he used a wooden pole as the stirrer, but this mixed the ingredients unequally and caused streaks to form. In 1805 he used a porous fireclay rod for the first time, and discovered that it not only kept the mass thoroughly mixed but also brought bubbles to the surface. Guinand later moved to Germany to take charge of a glassworks, and there he taught his new method to a young apprentice, Joseph Fraunhofer (1787–1826), who later became one of the greatest figures in the history of optics. Fraunhofer made accurate measurements of refractive indexes for different colors and found that with flint glass the results depended on the conditions of manufacture. Eventually, he made a refracting telescope with an objective of aperture 24 cm. that was sensibly free from aberrations. Its success completely changed the status of refracting telescopes, which now pushed reflectors almost entirely out of the picture. Fraunhofer's work so worried the British government that Michael Faraday and Sir John Herschel were asked to investigate the melting process. But their work was inconclusive, and the British industry began to recover only when Georges Bontemps, who had bought the secret of the process from Guinand's son, left France for political reasons in 1848 and joined the English firm of Chance Brothers.

So far, the main incentive for improving optical glass had come from astronomy. But as other sciences developed, microscopes grew in importance, and it was their defects that led to the next advance. In 1866 Carl Zeiss, a German instrument maker, began his collaboration with the physicist Ernst Abbe, who undertook research at the University of Jena to find ways of improving the quality of microscopes. One of his conclusions was that new types of glass were necessary, especially new flints and crowns for dealing with chromatic aberration without

causing other aberrations. In 1879 Abbe was sent samples of a new glass containing lithium, with a request that he should test its optical qualities. It turned out to be unsuitable for Abbe's purposes, but the incident served to bring Otto Schott, the man who had made the glass, into contact with Zeiss and Abbe, and before long Schott had moved to Jena and set up a glass factory. The association of instrument maker, physicist, and glassmaker proved enormously fruitful, and by the early 1900s the factory was manufacturing about 80 different optical glasses and had introduced into their mixtures 28 elements not previously used. (As a matter of fact the Rev. William Vernon Harcourt, in Britain, had investigated many of these new glasses some years earlier, but his work was never taken up by manufacturers.) The importance of Schott's work can be judged from the diagram on page 116, which is known as a *glass plot*. It is a plot of refractive index n against constringence V. The more different combinations of n and V there are, the more versatile the optical designer can become.

Photography was becoming popular at this time, and it presented designers with new problems. Cameras usually have a wide field of view, typically 50° as opposed to about 7° for field glasses and 1° for microscopes, and this means that certain aberrations (astigmatism, curvature of the field, and distortion) that are insignificant in telescopes and microscopes become important. The discovery of the new glasses played a large part in the history of photography. An idea of this is given by the diagram on page 117, showing how a lens called the *Goerz Dagor* was developed. This lens is an example of a *symmetrical anastigmat*, a type that owes its existence to the discovery of the new glasses.

In 1940 G. W. Morey, in the United States, introduced rare-earth oxides, especially those of lanthanum and thorium, into the melt, with the effect shown in the glass plot on page 116. In 1948 a continuous process for making optical glass was brought into use in the United States, where three firms—Corning, the Pittsburgh Plate Glass Company, and Bausch and Lomb—each developed their own form of a process that has in many countries largely replaced the method of manufacturing in batches. The

116

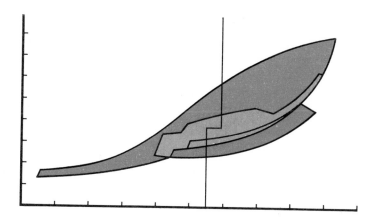

Above: the historical development of optical glasses. The optical
characteristics of a glass type are defined by its refractive index (n) and its
constringence, or reciprocal relative dispersion (V). A particular glass type may
therefore be represented by a single point on a plot of n against V. Before 1880
all the glasses available to lens designers lay in the area shown in blue. In that
year Otto Schott began to make new types of glass and by 1934 the known
types covered the additional area shown in gray. Since 1934 the red area
has also been filled in, largely due to the work of G. W. Morey and his colleagues
at the Eastman Kodak Company in the United States. A large part of this area,
especially in the more remote regions, contains glasses that have been made
only in the laboratory and are not manufactured commercially. The diagram also
shows the line dividing crowns from flints. This is a matter of convention, and the
accepted distinction lies in the size of relative dispersion rather than
refractive index.

Opposite: the development of photographic lenses. A common lens in the last
century was the rapid rectilinear (left), consisting of two identical achromatic
doublets on either side of a stop. Each doublet had a positive element of crown
glass and a negative one of flint. The symmetry of this construction
automatically reduced the aberrations called coma and distortion. The discovery
of barium crown glass by Otto Schott led to a modification of this lens, called
the Zeiss Protar (center), designed in 1890. The converging lens in the rear
component was replaced by one made of the new type of glass. Astigmatism
and curvature of the field were thus greatly reduced, but the advantages of
symmetry were lost and the lens suffered from spherical aberration. Two or
three years later these problems were largely overcome in the Goerz Dagor (right),
a lens still used today. Each half consists of a triplet. The refractive indexes rise
outward from the stop, the values being 1.52, 1.57, and 1.61, and the glasses
common crown, light flint, and dense barium crown, in that order.

latest development to affect glassmakers has been the use of electronic digital computers to aid lens designers in their calculations. Their power is so great that designers are finding they need *fewer* glass types than they used to. It is still necessary to have glasses with very different optical properties, spanning a wide area on the glass plot, but designers do not need so many glasses with only slightly different properties, lying close together on the plot.

While the quality of optical glass improved steadily, so did the methods of processing it. From the 17th century onward, better materials were continually being brought into use for the tools, *mallets* (glues for holding the lenses in place), abrasives, and polishes. One of the most important innovations, introduced as long ago as Newton's time, was the use of pitch as the polishing material. Machines for grinding and polishing first appeared early in the 17th century, and Chérubin d'Orléans describes several invented by himself to make the processes easier, faster, and more accurate.

The Manufacture of Optical Glass

The methods of making optical glass are similar in outline to those described in Chapter 4 for other kinds of glass, but much more careful control is necessary at every stage of the process. Small differences in chemical composition and heat treatment affect optical properties, and optical quality is bad unless the product is free from discoloration, striation, frozen-in strains, and chemical nonhomogeneity. The end-product is raw glass, which the manufacturer sells to be processed elsewhere.

The first stage of manufacture is mixing and melting the raw materials. These must be very pure, and especially free from anything that colors glass. The commonest coloring agents are iron

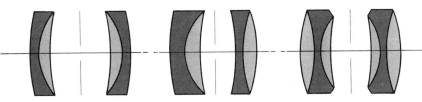

A lens-grinding machine from Manzini's Dioptrica Pratica *(1660). The blank was pressed down by hand onto the rotating concave tool at top left, to form a convex lens surface.*

oxides, Fe_2O_3 and FeO. In plate glass 0.05 per cent of iron oxide in the sand is acceptable; for most optical glass the amount is 0.01 per cent, while for special optical glasses it is about 0.001 per cent. This is why sand for optical purposes costs from 6 to 30 times as much as sand for window glass.

Until 1948 optical glass was melted in pot furnaces and produced in batches. In that year the continuous process first appeared, and is now used in many countries for quantities greater than 2000 kg. In this process, melting and the next two stages, refining and homogenizing, are carried out in one tank, each part of which is held at a constant temperature, set according to the action required. At the refining stage the glass is heated to about 1400°c in the case of flint, or 1550°c for crown, to remove bubbles of gas. Homogenizing is done by the stirring process invented by Guinand. This is followed by forming, when the glass is put into the shape in which it is sold. It can be rolled, or extruded like toothpaste into strips or panes, cast into blocks, or drawn into rods; for making lenses and prisms it is sometimes molded into approximately the right shape and supplied as a blank. These primary forming processes are continuous, and are followed by secondary processes such as remolding, sawing, or grinding, carried out by the purchaser of the raw glass.

After the primary forming process, the glass is annealed in such a way that no temperature differences greater than three or four degrees centigrade are allowed to exist within the glass. The cooling rate depends on the bulk of the article, ranging from less than 1°c per hour to 360°c per hour, so that annealing can take as long as two months. The heat treatment not only reduces stresses, but also acts as a precise control on the optical properties of the glass. Thus a special barium crown glass cooled at 20°c per day has a slightly higher refractive index (1.72000 as opposed to 1.71644) than one cooled at 360°c per hour.

The batch method of manufacture was carried out, until about 1930, in a ceramic pot holding roughly 1000 kg. of glass, and the melting, refining, and homogenizing took about 48 hours. After homogenizing, the pot was cooled slowly, the glass and pot were broken, and the pieces of glass were reheated and formed into slabs. The process was wasteful, as only 25 per cent of the contents of a pot was of acceptable quality. The present trend is toward using platinum crucibles instead of expendable ceramic pots. Platinum is expensive, but it is remarkably resistant to attack by molten glass so that the glass is unlikely to be contaminated by the refractory. Platinum was indeed used by Faraday in his researches, and the German firm of Schott (Mainz) have recently developed a continuous-casting process using a platinum tank.

Making Lenses and Prisms

The first step in making a lens is to prepare a blank suitable for grinding down. This may be simply a slightly oversize slab, in the shape of a square with the corners cut off. An old way of making a blank was to saw the glass with a metal wire fed with water and abrasive grit, such as emery or Carborundum. The grit was forced into contact with the glass and caused rolling abrasion. Small pieces of glass were fractured from the surface and washed away by the water. This method was slow, and in industrial workshops today blanks are usually cut out with a high-speed rotating disk whose edge is charged with Carborundum or diamond. Sometimes they are molded by the glass manufacturer, giving the advantages of continuous production and a blank close to the right shape. The disadvantage is that the glass is chilled as it is poured into the mold, producing strains that have to be removed carefully at the annealing stage.

The blank is then *rough-ground* to almost the required final shape and size. This can be done by hand, using a convex metal tool to make a concave glass surface and vice versa, or a flat

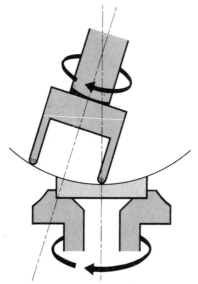

The curve-generator. Any ring can be placed against the inside or outside surface of a sphere of larger radius so that the two are in contact at every point of the ring's circumference. The curve-generator consists of a circular *cutting edge (the end of a cylindrical diamond lap)* used to cut a spherical *surface in glass, as shown here for a concave surface. The cutter rotates quickly while the lens, which is held in position by a vacuum, rotates more slowly. The lowest part of the cutting edge is at the center of the lens, on the lens axis. To produce a surface of different curvature the angle between the two axes of rotation is changed.*

tool to make a flat surface, with a suitable abrasive between the tool and the glass. This would rarely be done nowadays, and in modern factories the usual method is to use a curve-generator, whose principle is shown in the diagram on page 120.

This method can only produce *spherical* surfaces, and the same is true of the traditional grinding process. There is an interesting reason why spherical surfaces are the easiest ones to produce. Grinding can be looked upon as repeatedly sliding two surfaces over each other until all impediments to free motion have been broken away. This must be so when both surfaces are spherical, since only then can one slide over the other *in any direction* without resistance. Thus, if a roughly concave, irregular piece of iron is ground against a roughly convex piece, they become accurately spherical and matching, and can be used as tools to grind lenses on. Most high-quality lenses have spherical surfaces not because the spherical shape is ideal, but because it is the easiest one to produce accurately. (As a matter of fact, non-spherical lenses have been made since the 18th century but they cannot be manufactured both accurately and cheaply even now, because polishing always tends to make them spherical.) A flat

Above: concave blocks of lenses, showing the appearance of the surfaces when rough-ground (right) and when polished (left). Each block is carefully made up so that the upper faces of all the lenses are part of the same spherical surface. First, a button of pitch is stuck onto the rear surface of each lens. The front surfaces are wetted and all the lenses placed facedown onto a convex tool of the correct radius of curvature. The lenses are temporarily held in place by the water, with the buttons of pitch pointing outward. A warm concave tool is then pressed down onto them so that the pitch flows, spreads, and hardens, and when the concave tool is lifted it takes the lenses with it to form a block like those shown. The concave tool can then be fixed in position in the polishing machine. This is like the one shown on page 108 except that for concave surfaces the lenses are usually on top, moving over a rotating polisher.

Right: a block of lenses after polishing. The apparatus is the same as in the photograph on page 108, but here the surface of the polisher is visible, coated with pitch. Channels have been cut to allow for the pitch to flow. The pink color is due to cerium oxide, which is used as the polishing powder. At one time jeweler's rouge was commonly used, a reminder of the fact that lens polishing derives historically from jewel polishing.

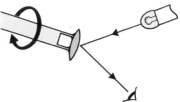

Above: optical centering. The lens is cemented onto the tubular end of a brass spindle. While the cement is still soft, the lens is adjusted until the reflection of the lamp no longer wobbles when the spindle is turned about its own axis on a lathe. The, optical axis of the lens then coincides with the axis of rotation.

Above left: This photograph shows mechanical centering, in which two identical metal tubes, very accurately lined up with each other, are pushed together to grip the lens between them so that the lens axis coincides with the common axis of the two tubes. The grinding wheel behind the lens then moves forward slightly and edges it, while water from the tube above cools it and washes away the glass particles. This method of centering is accurate only if the lens has fairly steep curves; otherwise the optical method is used.

surface is a special case of a spherical surface with infinite radius, and a flat tool can be made by grinding three pieces of metal against each other in turn until each one matches both of the others accurately. In practice, neither flat nor spherical tools are made by grinding metal against metal, but they are often given their final, accurate finish in this way.

Rough-grinding is done with fairly coarse abrasives and is followed by *fine-grinding*, or *smoothing*, in which finer abrasives are used. In mass production, it is possible to smooth several lenses at once. This is because they are all of the same size and shape after rough-grinding. They can therefore be mounted as shown on page 121—an operation called *blocking*—and ground

Above: A large number of identical prisms can be milled together when they are held in a jig, as shown in this photograph. The upper horizontal surfaces with a matt appearance have just been milled by causing the jig to move horizontally underneath a cylindrical diamond lap rotating about a vertical axis. It is evident from the photograph that this jig is designed for the manufacture of prisms of quite complicated shape.

Below: a jig for grinding prism angles to match the angles of a master prism. The master (A) and blank (B) are cemented onto the ends of a rigid shaft. This is rotated until each face of the master, in turn, is perpendicular to the axis of a sighting device (C), as detected by the fact that light sent down through it is reflected back along its own path. The workpiece is then machined by the cylindrical diamond lap. This method is used when very great accuracy is needed, or when the required number of prisms is not great enough to justify the cost of the kind of jig shown in the photograph above.

Below: Several prisms can be polished together, as shown, if they are blocked in plaster. The block is actually made upside down by standing the prisms facedown on a flat surface, surrounding them with a brass ring (shown here in black), pouring plaster over them, and allowing it to set.

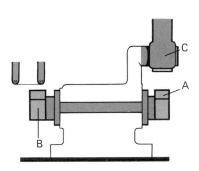

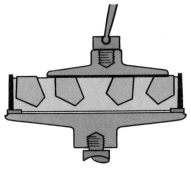

together as though they formed one large spherical surface. After smoothing, the surfaces are very finely ground and must be polished. This is done while the lenses are still blocked, as shown on pages 108 and 121. The lenses are then removed from the block, protected on the polished face, and blocked again to repeat the smoothing and polishing operation on the second surface.

The next processes are centering and edging. *Edging* means grinding around the rim to make the lens perfectly cylindrical and bring it down to the right diameter; this is fairly easy to do if the lens can be rotated about its own axis of symmetry. A grinding wheel is then brought up to the rim and a perfectly cylindrical edge is produced. Getting the lens to rotate about its own axis in the first place is the procedure known as *centering*, and two methods of doing this are illustrated on page 122. Finally, the lens is given a protective chamfering. Where the polished surface meets the rim there is a sharp corner that can be chipped easily, and this angle is therefore carefully ground to produce a beveled edge, or *chamfer*.

The stages of making a prism are the same as those for making a lens, with flat tools replacing the spherical ones. There is the additional problem of getting the angles right, and two ways of doing this are illustrated on page 123. For polishing several prisms at once, they can be blocked in plaster of paris, as shown on the same page.

The Mechanism of Grinding and Polishing

Although we know how to grind and polish glass, the nature of these processes is not clearly understood. Until this century they were thought to be essentially the same, the only difference being one of scale. According to this view, the particles of abrasive produced long scratches, or furrows, and the appearance of ground glass was due to the intersection of very many of these furrows running in different directions. At the polishing stage the width of these furrows was supposed to become much less than the wavelength of light.

We now believe that during grinding the particles of abrasive do not scratch the glass, but rather break little bits of it away to form pits. Modern theories of polishing fall into three broad groups. According to the first, the difference between grinding and polishing is that in the first process the backing to the abrasive is a hard material, such as iron, whereas in the second it is a soft one, such as pitch or felt. Because of this, the particles of polishing powder embed themselves in the backing and so plane the surface of the glass, cutting away a thickness of only a few molecules at a time. It has been claimed in support of this view that fine Carborundum, normally a grinding material, can be used for polishing if backed by a yielding material such as soft wood or cork.

Theories of the second group claim that the glass flows during polishing. One suggestion is that plastic flow occurs, with molecular bonds continually being broken and re-formed. This would require a strong force, which is available locally because the whole force between lens and polisher is concentrated at the few points where the glass makes contact with particles of rouge. An alternative explanation is that very high local pressures at these points produce high temperatures, so that the glass actually melts and flows as a liquid. One important piece of evidence for some kind of flow is that if the surface of polished glass is etched with hydrofluoric acid, so that the glass immediately below the surface comes into view, scratches made by the powder during polishing appear; indeed, a deep scratch can be made to disappear and reappear several times by alternately polishing and etching. Another piece of evidence is that it is possible to polish glass so that it does not lose any weight, which is interpreted as meaning that the glass flows but is not cut away at all. The idea that the flow is actually due to melting, as opposed to mechanical forces, is supported by experiments on the sliding of one metal surface over another. These showed that the temperature reached was just equal to the melting point of the metal. Furthermore, the metals could only be polished successfully if the melting point of the abrasive was higher than that of the metal, whereas the relative hardness of abrasive and metal was, rather surprisingly, not at all important. It is not certain that the polishing mechanism is the same for glass as for metals; but there is some evidence that glasspolishing also depends on the melting point of the powder as compared with the softening point of the glass.

The theories in the third group state that a chemical reaction takes place between the glass, the rouge, and the pitch. Most of them postulate that a layer of silica gel is repeatedly formed and swept away. The main evidence for the chemical theory is that polishing is greatly speeded by the presence of water, which is believed to hydrolize the glass.

It may well be that more than one mechanism can be used to give glass a polish, and that under normal conditions several are at work. There is strong evidence that each of the processes postulated does take place—glass certainly *can* flow plastically, for instance—but it does not follow that the process helps polishing. Glasspolishing, by definition, occurs beyond the scope of the optical microscope, and the great surge of research into it only began with the invention of the electron microscope and phase-contrast techniques, aided by the growing understanding of the properties of solid surfaces.

Other Optical Uses of Glass

Prisms and lenses are not the only optical components. Our precision technology rests on the existence of the *optical flat*, the standard of flatness by which tools and gauges are judged. It consists of a disk of glass, typically 10 centimeters across, with a surface flat to 0.02 micron. The fact that glass can be shaped so accurately derives from its liquid nature, since there is no crystal structure or grain imposing itself on the surface. Optical flats are made in much the same way as lenses. The tools must be flat, but it is an interesting fact that they do not need to be nearly as accurately flat as the work they are producing. An experienced glasspolisher constantly checks the flatness of his work against a standard flat, using an interferometer, and he can use his imperfectly flat polishing tool to correct small deviations from flatness. The standard flat itself is made by polishing three pieces of glass against each other in turn until each pair of them matches exactly, which is only possible when they are all flat.

Quite a large part of the production of optical glass goes into the making of *reticles*, or *graticules*—glass disks engraved with fine lines, used in the eyepieces of optical instruments. The engraving may be a scale for measuring the size of the image,

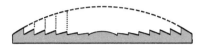

To keep down the weight of very large lenses they are sometimes made in a saw-tooth form. These Fresnel lenses *are not used if the formation of an accurate image is required, but they are used, for instance, in lighthouses.*

or it may simply be a setting mark. It is viewed under strong magnification, so that the lines must be fine and accurately placed. The image is seen through the glass, which must be free from blemishes. The marks are produced either by scribing with a diamond mounted in a machine or by etching with hydrofluoric acid, using wax to protect the rest of the glass surface.

Glass used for optical purposes need not always be of very good optical quality. For instance, the lens of a lighthouse is not used to form an image but to concentrate the rays into a powerful beam, and need not be made of high-quality glass, because great accuracy is not required. Lighthouse lenses are often made in the form of *Fresnel lenses*, as in the diagram on page 127.

A good example of the use of nonoptical glass for very accurate optical work is the objective mirror of a large reflecting telescope. Since the time of Fraunhofer, telescope designers have switched back to mirrors for the objectives, because of the difficulty of making very large glass disks of uniform optical quality. The glass in such a mirror need not be of optical quality for the simple reason that the light does not pass through it; unlike domestic mirrors, a telescope objective is metallized on its *front* surface. During the 19th century, great improvements were made in methods of depositing thin films of metal onto glass, with the result that glass has now come to be preferred as the material for mirrors—it can be shaped very accurately, takes a high polish, and has very little tendency to warp or distort with age. Thermal expansion is kept low in telescope mirrors by making them of Pyrex glass. Another problem is that large disks bend under their own weight, and the 500-cm. mirror at Mt. Palomar was therefore constructed in the form of a thin face supported on a honeycomb structure also made of glass. This mirror, the largest in the world, is one of the glassmaker's most spectacular achievements.

6 Commercial and Industrial Glass

Optical components account for only a very small fraction of the total output of the modern glass industry. In the United States, for example, optical glass accounts for less than four per cent of the total value of annual glass production (1963). The overwhelming bulk of glass produced may be termed industrial and commercial glass. This heading includes not only the more obvious applications such as windows and containers of all kinds, but, increasingly, many items that represent new and imaginative applications of the material. The versatility of glass is in fact being continually demonstrated and, while it is true that many new materials have recently invaded fields that once seemed to be the natural preserves of the glassmaker, it is equally true that glass today is doing jobs previously done by very different materials. In addition, entirely new forms of glass have appeared, which are able to perform tasks that are themselves new and that no other material could perform. To give only one example, more than 500 different kinds of glass are at present being

Borosilicate glass, because it is suitably heat resistant and chemically inert, is used for the massive pipes in which waste gases from a chlorination plant are purified, or "scrubbed," by passing through water. The pieces of clay stacked in the pipes simply act as mixers for water and gases.

made and used commercially in the United Kingdom alone. The four principal markets for glass are the packaging, building, engineering, and electrical industries. To satisfy them the commercial glass maker, like the optical glass maker, must produce a great variety of goods, each with the best possible combination of thermal, mechanical, chemical, and electrical characteristics for its particular purpose.

Glass Packaging

So successfully has the glass industry met competition from the new synthetic materials in the field of packaging that in the United States glass-container production doubled between 1949 and 1963, reaching a figure of about 25,000 million containers a year. In Britain production increased from 280 million a year in 1913 to 5000 million (or 13.7 million per day) in 1965. Similar growth in output has taken place in most European countries. Continuous, high-speed methods of making and filling bottles of all kinds have enabled manufacturers to match demand and to keep prices down. Research, too, has shown and is showing ways in which the mechanical strength and chemical resistance of glass containers can be greatly improved.

What are the physical requirements of glass containers that must be taken into account in the design and manufacture of bottles? Briefly, these are mechanical strength, thermal strength, and chemical resistance. Mechanical strength, which is especially important in the case of multitrip (or returnable) bottles, means the ability of the bottles to stand up to internal pressure, vertical loads (such as that exerted by a capping machine), and sudden impact. Potentially, glass should be immensely strong, but, as we have seen, its theoretical strength of 70,000 kg/cm^2 is never approached. Thin and exceptionally perfect glass fibers can withstand tensile loads of the order of 15,000 kg/cm^2, but with new bulk glass the tensile strength is not likely to exceed 1500 kg/cm^2 and after being used only a few times, it is likely to fall to around 400 kg/cm^2. This loss of strength is primarily due to *microcracks*—tiny imperfections in the surface that are present in any glass article no matter how carefully it is made, and that can be aggravated by abrasion and even atmospheric action. Any progress toward the "unbreakable" bottle must therefore be directed at eliminating, or at least minimizing, the effects of these flaws. Glass surfaces can be temporarily protected by lubrication techniques: Silicones, waxes, and other substances have been used commercially, but they make the bottles slippery to handle and the labels more likely to slip off. The thermal toughening process that was described in Chapter 4 is useful for strengthening flat glass but cannot easily be applied to bottles, and the chemical toughening processes based on ion exchange, which will be dealt with in the final chapter, are too long and expensive to be used with cheap mass-produced articles.

The manufacturers have had to find another answer. In Great Britain, United Glass Ltd. have already made many millions of bottles by a production-line process that has been developed from experiments on the diffusion of various metallic compounds into glass. They call the process Titanizing, and it is carried out in a special chamber at the hot end between the bottle machine and the annealing lehr. While the bottles are still red-hot they are sprayed with an organic compound of titanium; this has the property that on striking the hot glass it decomposes into a volatile part, which simply evaporates away, and a layer of titanium oxide, which is left on the glass. By this means the layer is made so thin that the treated glass remains transparent, and the effect is permanent because titanium oxide is slightly soluble in glass. Titanized glass is durable and extremely resistant to the formation of microcracks, and bottles that have been treated in this way are well equipped to withstand the jostling that they receive during their normal working lives. The fact that glass-to-glass friction is greatly reduced in this way ensures a longer life by freeing bottles from one of the chief causes of abrasion scars.

The results in terms of improved bursting strength are impressive. One curious fact is that bottles of irregular shape, which as we shall see presently are inherently weaker, gain most from the process. With bottles of simple round section, bursting strengths are increased by about 50 per cent, but with the more complex, basically weaker shapes, the strength is often more than doubled.

In theory, the best shape of glass container for withstanding internal pressure would be spherical, since this shape allows for the even distribution of pressure and expansion. However, spherical bottles are impractical for other reasons, such as the awkwardness of storing them, and so the cylindrical shape is preferred. This is more practical, and still symmetrical enough to withstand pressure well. If the corners at base or neck are well rounded, they too will withstand pressure well, but flat sides will tend to move outward more readily and so concentrate most of the tensile stress on their outer surfaces.

We know that glass is capable of resisting very severe compression, so the problem of vertical load strength is not a great one. Different shoulder shapes provide widely varying strengths, and by taking into account the mechanical filling and capping operation for which a given bottle is planned, the designer can select his shape accordingly. Resistance to impact is a much more difficult quality to test and measure; at the same time it is extremely important in the modern bottling plant, since breakages

This complete bottling unit decrates, washes, fills, caps, and recrates 200 bottles per minute. Bottles must be strong enough to withstand the jostling and friction inevitable with such machines, since breakages are costly not only in themselves, but also in the delays they cause.

on the production line are costly—not only in themselves, but in the delays they cause. As a general rule, the thicker the glass wall, the greater the resistance; but as weight is always a vital consideration in packaging, the designer naturally aims at the best possible combination of lightness and strength. Attempts to reduce the weight of glass containers, based on research into strength and design factors, have had considerable success during the last few decades. In 1930 an ordinary half-pint beer bottle could weigh as much as 400 gm.; today bottles of this kind weigh about 300 gm., and are just as strong and durable.

Mechanical strength usually increases with weight; thermal strength—the ability of a container to withstand sudden changes in temperature—moves in the opposite direction. Temperature difference causes tension in the colder surface and compression in the hotter surface, resulting in fracture. The thinner the glass wall of a container, the more difficult it is to establish a large temperature difference between the two surfaces, and so the less

A glass jar with internal stresses (left) and one in which annealing has removed such stresses, photographed in polarized light through a filter and analyzer. This shows how the effects of different kinds of forces on jars of various designs can be assessed with a view to making them lighter.

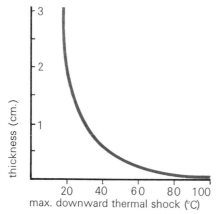

Theoretical relation between the wall thickness of glass containers and the maximum downward thermal shock they can withstand. Breakage due to thermal shock almost always occurs on the outside surface of the container, since the inner surface, irrespective of wall thickness, can take a drop of over 100°C.

thickness (cm.)

max. downward thermal shock (°C)

likely the glass is to break. The diagram on page 134 gives an idea of the theoretical relation between the wall thickness and the thermal shock resistance. Notice that the thermal shock given in the graph is a downward one: The amount of tension produced in the surface of a bottle by sudden chilling is about twice as great as that caused by sudden heating, which means that the maximum sudden increase in temperature that the bottle can stand is about twice the corresponding sudden decrease. The diagram shows the more critical case. Because thermal resistance decreases with wall thickness, a large glass container is generally more vulnerable than a small one. Bottle shape, too, has an important effect upon thermal resistance, because the bending effects of the stresses caused by temperature change are much greater where base and sidewall join; for this reason nearly all modern bottle design allows for a gentle curve at this point.

The mechanical strength of a glass bottle or jar can be improved by making its surface extremely resistant to the formation of microcracks and by judicious design; its resistance to heat shock, too, can be improved by careful design. Now we come to the problem of chemical attack. All materials react upon each other in different ways, but for most purposes glass containers can be looked upon as completely inert—that is, able to store any liquid or solid indefinitely without deteriorating. It is this property of glass that makes it such an ideal material for packaging of all kinds. Many bottles, however, require especially high resistance to chemical attack: for example, bottles used in the pharmaceutical industry for storing corrosive acids. Reduction of the alkali content of the batch does much to make the glass more resistant, but this also raises the melting point of the glass and makes forming difficult. For this reason a more elaborate process is adopted. The interior of the finished bottle is filled with the acid gases sulfur dioxide and sulfur trioxide, which remove most of the sodium from the inner surface of the container. This process of replacement by rapid diffusion produces a layer inside the container that is more resistant chemically than the body of the glass; at the same time it removes the possibility that the glass will deteriorate later through sodium loss. Glass of this kind is called *sulfated* glass, and its chemical resistance is up to a hundred times that of ordinary untreated glass in the storing of extremely alkali-sensitive drugs.

Modern nonstop mass-production methods make it possible to produce glass containers in enormous numbers at remarkably low cost. The total annual production of handmade bottles in Britain in 1700, for example, was around 3 million; now, with round-the-clock working, the figure is in the region of 14 million per day, and the nominal cost of a mass-produced small bottle is as little as a penny. It is the combination of efficiency, cheapness, and eye-appeal that makes glass an ideal material for containers. A good example is quoted by B. E. Moody in his book *Packaging in Glass*: When prepared baby foods were first produced in the United States in 1926 they were put into tins; by 1939, 13 per cent of all baby foods produced in the U.S. were packed in glass, 75 per cent by 1957, 80 per cent by 1960, and almost 100 per cent by 1963. The largest producer of baby food in the United States has attributed this trend almost entirely to consumer preference.

Glass in Building

In 1900 the only glass used in building the average house went into making the windows. Today glass is used for nearly every kind of architectural purpose, and structures whose surfaces consist of up to 90 per cent glass are fairly common. Glass in almost every imaginable form—plate and sheet glass, wired, ribbed, and patterned glass, thermally toughened glass, translucent glass blocks, and the various forms of decorative glass such as glass mosaic, fused glass, and slab glass used with concrete—provides new means of enriching buildings.

Much of the glass used in modern buildings is in the form of flat glass. The application of continuous methods of manufacture during the last few decades has had a valuable impact upon the efficiency and economy of the flat-glass industry, and has enabled the makers of ordinary annealed flat glass—whether sheet, rolled, or float—to keep costs down. The higher cost of toughened and laminated glasses has prevented them from being widely used in buildings except for special applications, such as all-glass doors, where ordinary glass would not have great enough strength or resistance to the effects of climate. As a rule, vertically drawn sheet glass is used wherever through vision is required, as long as some slight distortion is acceptable in the interests of economy. Similarly, rolled or roughcast glass is used where clear vision is not essential, while figured rolled glass, upon one surface of which a pattern or texture has been impressed, is used for internal partitions, or windows of rooms where partial or total privacy is required. Shatterproof wired glass, in which electrically welded wire netting is inserted during manufacture, was first used in the 19th century, and is used for glazed roofs and canopies where falling glass might be a danger. Moreover, in case of fire, this kind of glass is less likely to break under heat and so allow free passage to the flames than is ordinary annealed flat glass of similar thickness. During World War II many buildings were saved from destruction by incendiary bombs by the fire-retarding properties of this type of glass. Float or polished plate glass is used wherever windows or partitions are required to give clear undistorted vision as a first priority.

An important use of glass in building is as preformed hollow blocks. These each consist of two molded halves accurately fused together to make a complete unit. During sealing, the air inside expands with the intense heat so that when the block is closed and cooled the captive air contracts, producing a partial vacuum. The blocks are not load-bearing, but when laid in mortar have a minimum compressive strength of 30–40 kg/cm^2 of gross loaded area, which is more than the compressive strength of normal masonry. Because of their patterned surfaces they are translucent, transmitting about 75 per cent of the light passing through two thicknesses of plate glass equivalently spaced, and they are capable of cutting down noise by as much as 40 decibels. They are frequently used for external and internal walls, staircase lights, and panels, and for any situation where a combination of diffused light and privacy is required.

Double-glass insulation is another development that has come about as a direct response to the requirements of the building industry. A window, instead of being a single pane of glass, consists of two parallel panes with a sealed air space in between. This has the considerable advantage that the inner pane keeps comparatively warm even when the outside pane is extremely cold, and fuel savings of up to 36 per cent have been achieved. In addition, double glazing prevents condensation and misting with normal room temperature (20°C) until the outside temperature reaches –32°C. In some countries, units of sealed double glazing are available in standard sizes, and have done much to

The increasing use of glass, especially in combination with steel frameworks, has transformed the appearance of cities. Structures of up to 90 per cent glass in surface area are not uncommon.

Translucent hollow glass blocks. These allow light to be evenly distributed to the rooms beyond and are used when diffused light and privacy are required.

Glass-fiber matting being laid in a domestic attic. The result in a centrally heated house will be a saving of up to 30 per cent in fuel costs.

The boilerhouse of a car factory. Hot-water pipes are insulated with rigid preformed glass-fiber matting, finished with a hard-setting composition.

make rooms more habitable by stopping down drafts, reducing heat loss by conduction, and restricting the formation of window condensation.

Another recent trend is the increasing use of glass claddings in buildings. Opaque, toughened glass is bonded and mechanically anchored to one surface of a lightweight concrete slab to produce a glass-faced load-bearing brick. Such bricks are made in many colors and finishes; they are extremely durable and will often outlast the building on which they are used. They are fire-resistant and half the weight of other materials of similar strength (such as cast stone), and they provide two or three times as much insulation as the equivalent thickness of uncladded brick or cast stone.

Many of the glass products used in building are made from glass in the form of fiber. Fibers compressed into wool are used as insulation against heat and cold, as a filtering medium, as a sound-absorbent material, as electrical insulation, and as a decorative fabric. For heat, cold, and sound insulation this glass wool, either in plain or paper-faced mats, in rigid boards, in preformed molded sections, or in wire-backed quilt, is used in industrial, commercial, domestic, and agricultural buildings. As thermal insulation, this wool has a number of advantages over alternative materials: It has low heat conductivity, small heat capacity, and exceptional resistance to weathering, and does not corrode in contact with metals such as steel or aluminum. Among the most important uses of glass fibers is domestic and industrial pipe insulation, where it is suitable for use at pipe temperatures up to 600°c.

Perhaps the most interesting application of glass fiber in building is in the reinforcement of plastics, producing for the architect and designer a whole new group of materials with properties never before available together. The main advantages of fiber-reinforced plastics are: high strength-to-weight ratio, any required degree of translucency, almost unlimited freedom of shape, fire resistance, and a wide range of easily maintained colors and finishes. In addition, the first of these properties means that large prefabricated units molded from fiber-reinforced plastic are still light enough to be easily handled, which can do much to speed construction and cut cost. The simplest fiber-reinforced plastic laminate uses chopped strands of randomly deposited glass fibers to reinforce polyester resin. On a weight-for-weight basis this material has about twice the tensile strength of structural steel, and can withstand up to four times the compressive load. By increasing the amount of glass fiber and by using pressure molding, plastics can be made that provide as much as 14 times the tensile strength of the equivalent weight of steel.

Already architects are making use of these moldings in a number of ways. Translucent dome lights, opaque ventilator cowls and rainwater guttering are used on the outsides of buildings, while applications inside include doors and screens, water tanks and lids, shower cubicles, hand basins, and baths. Standardized fiber-reinforced plastic units are already available, including corrugated translucent sheeting, which combines advantages of light weight, resistance to impact, ease of fixing, and good

Glass, which is relatively transparent to sunlight but retains the longwave heat radiation re-radiated by plants, benches, etc., is invaluable to market gardeners. Double glazing, because of its superior heat conservation, is increasingly widely used.

weathering properties. Similarly, small structures such as telephone kiosks, domestic swimming pools, public conveniences, shelters at bus-stops, and outdoor chairs and benches can all be mass-produced by molding. Another important application in connection with the more conventional construction materials is in the molds used for casting concrete units. Molds made of fiber-reinforced plastic, which require no greasing to ensure easy release for the concrete when formed, give the units absolute uniformity and an extremely smooth finish. Applications like these, however, are far from exploiting the true potential of this material, whose full value in the building industry has not yet been realized.

Another way in which glass has found effective use in building is in the transparent mirror, which acts as a mirror or as a window depending upon the relative intensity of the light on either side. Someone looking through it from a darkened room into a well-lit one sees it as a window; viewed from the well-lit room it acts as a mirror. To obtain this effect, plate glass is given a chromium alloy film about 0.0000001 cm. thick by vacuum sputtering. Among the numerous uses already found for this strange material are observation panels in nursery walls, clinics, hospitals, and zoos, security windows in banks, post offices, and stores, and some television equipment.

A useful material called *foam glass* is made by heating a mixture of ground glass and finely divided carbon in a mold until the heated mixture rises like a cake and fills the mold. When cooled and taken out, the "cake" is a mass of sealed glass bubbles, rigid but extremely light and buoyant. In this it resembles cork, and is even better than cork for a variety of uses—thermal insulation in refrigerators, building walls and roofs, and for life preservers and rafts. It is, in effect, synthetic lava.

One specialized area of building in which glass plays an invaluable part is the heated greenhouses used by most market gardeners. Double glazing, though expensive to install, is gradually becoming popular with growers because of its superior heat conservation, resulting in considerable cuts in heating costs. Light transmission is reduced by as much as 10 per cent by the addition of a second layer of glass, but growers have found that the amount of heat conserved and the resulting fuel saving fully make up for this loss of light. Many have found that non-hermetically sealed double glazing, which is generally much cheaper, ensures adequate saving to justify its use. Transparent plastics have been preferred by some growers, but whereas glass is relatively transparent to the shortwave radiation of sunlight and retains in the greenhouse the longer-wave heat radiation re-radiated by the plants, benches, etc., plastic transmits both kinds of radiation and therefore fails to trap the heat of the sun's rays. Experiments with cloches have shown that during the same period under adjacent glass and plastic equipment, the temperature under glass averaged a maximum of 25°c and a minimum of

The 11-m.-long mural at the Head Office of Pilkington Brothers Limited, made of fused laminates of colored, clear, and toughened glass, and plastic.

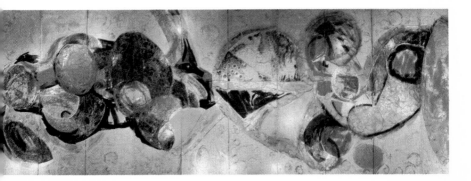

142

5°C compared with a maximum of 20°C and a minimum of 4°C for plastic. Some success has been achieved with an especially devised type of glass called *diffusing glass*, on which patterned rollers place an irregular undulating surface. When installed in greenhouses, it diffuses the sunlight in such a way as to reduce the total area of shadow inevitably cast by the opaque framework of the building.

There are many ways in which glass is used to decorate buildings, the most famous being the stained-glass windows that have been made for over a thousand years for churches and cathedrals. A few specialized firms survive that make true stained glass, but a great deal of glass is used in modern building today that is merely painted. More interesting, because they make use of the very structure of the material, are the results of recent experiments in a wide range of glass mosaic, glass set in concrete, and fused glass. Of these, glass mosaic is the simplest form of glass decoration and probably the cheapest. Pieces of colored glass, large or small, are stuck to a basic sheet of $\frac{1}{2}$-cm. plate glass with a transparent adhesive. The cracks between can be left as a fine network of white lines or filled with black cement. Murals, screens, and exhibition features can be achieved by this method. The combination of glass slabs and concrete has been used with success in France and the United States and is being more widely adopted. In this method, 2 cm. thick slabs are cut and faceted to catch the light and are then set in concrete to produce, on a larger scale, the effect of stained glass. The method is well suited for modern concrete churches. The fused-glass technique requires considerable skill in handling the different thermal expansion rates of various glasses. One of the best examples is the mural at the headquarters of Pilkington Brothers Limited of St. Helens, England, which is lit from behind to provide a magnificent array of shapes and colors.

Glass in Engineering

The demands of the engineering industry have probably brought about more of the recent advances in glass technology than those of any other users. The manufacture of automobiles, aircraft, ships, and boats involves some of the most complex and sophisticated uses of glass, and the needs of the industry have been met by such developments as laminated and toughened safety glass, wired glass, curved safety glass, fiber-glass insulation, and fiber-reinforced plastics. Again and again, when the designers of automobiles and supersonic aircraft have come up against the problems involved in providing visibility, safety, and insulation of all kinds, the makers of glass have undertaken the necessary research and found the answers.

Laminated safety glass was specifically developed by John Wood in England, and by Edouard Bénédictus in France, to cut down the many appalling disfigurements caused by road accidents in the early years of this century. In spite of its relatively high cost (about two and a half times that of toughened glass) it is still widely used for windshields and rear windows. Indeed in some countries its use in cars is compulsory. Most of the safety glass fitted in automobiles today, however, is toughened glass, which was first used in this way in the 1930s. When this glass breaks, the whole sheet shatters into fragments, but these fragments stay together in one piece. What the driver sees is his windshield disintegrating into a network of cracks. There is still the disadvantage that the windshield becomes almost completely opaque, and to overcome this, Triplex Safety Glass of Great Britain introduced zone-toughened windshields in 1961. These incorporate a modified zone about 40 cm. wide and 15 cm. deep directly in front of the driver's eyes. The glass within this area is toughened differently from the rest by adjusting the rate and method of quenching, so that when shattered it forms into larger fragments, which still give a considerable degree of visibility. A further improvement is to use toughened glass in which alternating strips have had the modified process applied to them. This makes for greater visibility on fracture and also greater consistency in the fracture pattern over the windshield as a whole.

The design of windshields for use in aircraft presented glass-makers with one of their most complex problems. For use in supersonic aircraft they must combine a number of exceptional properties: They must give unrestricted vision to the pilot, resist extremes of temperature ranging between $-80°C$ and $+150°C$ (caused by high altitude flying and kinetic heating respectively), and must also be able to stand up to the impact of birds flying into them when the aircraft is taking off or flying at low altitudes. For fighter aircraft, the windshields must also be proof against bullets. Most aircraft windshields, therefore, consist of laminated sheets of toughened glass, thus combining the advantages of both processes. An extra-thick layer of vinal is incorporated, usually between $\frac{1}{3}$ and $\frac{2}{3}$ cm. thick, and the edge of the windshield is often reinforced with a thin alloy strip. When a $\frac{2}{3}$-cm. interlayer is used the screen is proof against birds weighing up to 2 kg. traveling at a relative speed of 260 km/h; a 1-cm. layer is proof against birds weighing up to 8 kg. at similar speeds. For a bullet-proof composition several thicknesses of glass are laminated together, four thicknesses of toughened glass with a total thickness of 4 cm. providing protection against a 7.5-mm. bullet fired from a distance of 100 m. The problems of extremes of temperature can of course be overcome to some extent by using a form of double glazing, but the whole problem is further complicated by the formation of ice and frost at high altitudes. Double glazing, though successful in preventing misting, will not prevent or remove ice forming on the outer pane. To meet this problem the inner surface of the laminated glass is given a transparent layer of gold film 0.0000005 cm. thick, which may be heated electrically.

Electrically wired glass panels, too, are widely used against ice and frost in both aircraft and automobiles. These are made of laminated glass in which the heating wires, two thousandths of

Curved windows, heat-absorbing glass throughout, and laminated and electrically heated windshield and rear window are features of this especially designed "safety" car.

a centimeter thick, are embedded in the interlayer. The wires are crimped in such a way that they do not cause dazzle in sunlight. Heated backlights of this kind are now standard equipment on a number of automobile models in the colder parts of Europe and North America.

In hotter climates the heat and glare of the sun is a bigger problem than icing, and glasses that exclude infrared radiation are required. A trace of ferrous oxide increases the absorption of ultraviolet and infrared in the glass, and the resulting greenish tint is visible only from the outside. In thicknesses of $\frac{2}{3}$ and $\frac{1}{2}$ cm. the transmission of visible light is between 75 and 80 per cent, while heat transmission is reduced by about 50 per cent.

Glass-fiber-wool matting provides good heat and sound insulation because it traps air between its fibers. Efficiency depends upon the fineness of the fibers used, and matting consisting of fibers ranging in diameter from 0.00017 to 0.00034 cm. is widely used in the specialized fields of aircraft, marine, and automobile insulation. In passenger aircraft the problems of reducing noise inside and of temperatures as low as $-50°$c outside make insulation a necessity, and the fact that glass-fiber insulation can weigh as little as 300 gm/m^2 makes it ideal. Similarly, in modern passenger ships the efficient working of air-conditioning requires extensive insulation of the hull, super-structure, and ventilating shafts. Noise control, too, is a major problem in both cabins and engine spaces. The finer grades of glass-fiber wool are specified not only for passenger ships, but also for a great number of cargo ships and tankers. This material is also used on liquid-gas storage tanks, where the insulation must stand up to compression caused by the thermal movement of the container. Each tank is protected by thick resilient blankets that give 100 per cent recovery from frequent compression and are unaffected by temperatures as low as $-180°$c. In the automobile industry the smaller, high-revving engines and lighter bodies now being used make sound insulation increasingly important, and gearbox housings, tappet blocks, bulkheads, hoods, roofs, trunks, and floors are frequently fitted with molded pads made of glass fiber.

Numerous engineering applications have been found for glass-fiber-reinforced plastic. Intensive research has resulted in the combination of these two materials in a wide range of articles from chairs and chimney stacks to hulls for sailing boats. In the last of these, the molding industry has kept pace with development and it is now possible to produce hulls for large, specialized boats in small quantity as well as those for small standard dinghies. Such is the confidence of boat-builders in boats made in this way that a two-year guarantee is quite normal, which compares favorably with the standard one-year guarantee on a timber boat. Such confidence is not surprising when we remember that the compressive strength of glass-fiber-reinforced plastic is more than 10 times that of plywood and 50 per cent greater than that of the metal alloys normally used for boat hulls. The success of glass fiber in this field is impressive: At the annual London Boat Show in 1955, for example, reinforced plastic accounted for 4 per cent of the exhibits; in 1965, 47 per cent were built of this material.

Other applications of fiber-reinforced plastic in ·the field of engineering are numerous and steadily increasing. Entire and even chassis-less bodies for automobiles and other motor vehicles are becoming common, but among the more unexpected applications are shields for large generators and corrosion-resistant fume-stacks for chemical factories. As we have seen in the previous section, many prefabricated units such as domestic swimming pools, which lie between the industries of building and engineering, are made of fiber-reinforced plastic. The possibilities of this combination of glass and plastic seem almost limitless.

Glass would be even more useful than it is in engineering if it remained hard at very high temperatures. The more silica a given glass contains the higher its service temperature is, so that a glass consisting entirely of silica would offer the highest service temperature. Unfortunately, a number of snags prevent the large-scale manufacture of such glass at reasonable cost from being a practical proposition. The melting point of a glass consisting of 100 per cent silica is in the region of 1710°c, which is well above the range of ordinary commercial furnaces. In addition the removal of bubbles forming at such a temperature presents further problems, while high viscosity makes such a glass almost impossible to work by conventional methods. The answer to this problem was patented by two Americans, H. P. Hood and M. E. Nordberg of Corning Glass Works, during the last war. It is to use certain borosilicate glasses that are molded in the usual way, and then to soak the formed article in hydrochloric or sulfuric acid at around 98°c. This has the effect of leaching out the non-silicate ingredients, leaving the article as a skeleton with a multiplicity of tiny pores. When the article is then washed and dehydrated at high temperature, it shrinks in volume by about 30 per cent, and the pores close, leaving a transparent, non-porous glass. This is known as 96 per cent silica glass, and is almost pure fused silica. Because of the way in which it is made, it is sometimes called "shrunken glass." Although considerably more expensive than soda-lime or borosilicate glass, this offers a maximum service temperature between 1100° and 1200°c (compared with 460°c for soda-lime, 500°c for borosilicate, and

A 23-m. boat hull made of glass-fiber-reinforced plastic, after removal from the mold. The compressive strength of this composite material makes it ideal for the purpose.

around 650°C for alumino-silicate glasses) and can be used regularly at around 800°C. Its remarkably low thermal expansion coefficient enables this high-silica glass to withstand very severe heat shocks. Among the spectacular applications for this range of heat-resistant glasses are nose cones for missiles, and windows and antenna shields for space vehicles. Laboratory glassware, too, whenever the heat resistance required justifies the extra expense, is made of this type of glass.

Genuine fused silica, which is more than 99.5 per cent pure, is available for special purposes, and even higher purity silica glass can be made by high-temperature hydrolysis of silicon tetrachloride. The products of this process are pure silicon dioxide and hydrochloric acid, the first of which condenses out as a disk of high-optical-quality non-crystalline glass, while the HCl simply passes off as vapor. The impurity level in a glass made in this way may be as low as one part per hundred million. This is the most transparent of all glasses, transmitting the whole optical spectrum from the vacuum ultraviolet to the near infrared. In addition, because small gas molecules of helium and hydrogen, which cannot penetrate other glass types, diffuse easily through high-purity silica glass, it can be used to make molecular sieves for separating helium from natural gas. The same material is also extremely efficient at transmitting ultrasonic elastic waves with little distortion or absorption; this quality, as we shall see later, means that it can be used for making the acoustical delay lines used in computers and other electronic equipment.

Electrical Uses

Wherever electricity is used—in lighting, power transmission, communications, and the wide new fields of electronics—glass is used too. It is no exaggeration to say that without glass, many of the applications of electricity would be impossible. Nor is it surprising that in the United States, for example, glass items for all electrical and electronics purposes account for approximately 40 per cent of the value of all glass products.

Glass and the special products derived from it are well suited to electrical applications for a number of reasons. First, the properties of glass types can be varied easily over a wide range, making it possible to design a type for any particular purpose. Secondly, these properties can be precisely regulated and held. Thirdly, glass is relatively cheap to make and easy to form, with a high degree of precision and speed. The electrical properties of glass are: high dielectric strength, high volume resistivity, high surface resistivity and hard smooth surfaces that do not carbonize or become conductive under the action of arcs, a range of dielectric constants, and low power factor.

At temperatures below 100°C all glasses are fairly good insulators, and some of them are among the best insulating materials known. The surface of glass will conduct electricity if water is absorbed in it, but if this is prevented by a water-repelling agent such as one of the silicone liquids, the volume resistivity of glass can be as high as 10^{19} ohm-cm. This property naturally depends largely on the composition of the glass, and it can be as low as 10^8 ohm-cm. in some types of glass. Moreover, as with all good insulating materials, the resistivity of glass decreases with rising temperature; when heated to 1200°–1400°C its specific resistance may be as low as 100 ohm-cm. This makes it possible to melt glass electrically simply by passing electricity through the glass itself. Also, we have seen that glass can be given a thin metallic coating so that its surface conducts electricity. Coated glass panels are now being made in various sizes and shapes, for domestic and industrial heating.

One of the basic requirements of electrical lighting is that the source of light must be contained in a transparent or translucent envelope, or bulb, that is impermeable, unaffected by gas, vapor, or liquid, and has a high electrical resistivity. It must be possible to join the envelope easily to metal, and the whole must be suitable for mass production at low cost. In special circumstances the material used must be resistant to certain chemicals and very high temperatures: Glass admirably fills all these requirements. Glass envelopes for the electric bulb or fluorescent tube can be made from cheap soda-lime compositions; special compositions have been developed for special uses, such as envelopes for high-pressure mercury lamps and sodium discharge lamps, or solder glasses for sealing glass to metal. When the temperature conditions demand it, as when rain or snow on the hot glass surface would cause fracture, heat-resisting borosilicate glasses have to be employed. This material has about one third the expansion of ordinary lime glass, greater resistance to heat shock, and excellent chemical stability.

The large-scale joining of glass to metal, though occasionally used in the past for decorative purposes, is in fact a fairly recent development, first used commercially by the electrical lamp industry. Glass is fused to metals at temperatures of about 1100°C or more in order that a thin film of oxide may form. This, being soluble in both glass and metal, serves as a cement between the two. However, any difference between the coefficients of thermal expansion of the glass and the metal will set up stresses as the seal cools, and these stresses must be below the breaking strength of both or the seal will crack. Platinum was the first sealing metal used, because its thermal expansion was known to be similar to that of the glass then used, and it was already familiar to scientists because of its use in connection with glass in laboratory work on the conduction of electricity. Unfortunately, platinum is an extremely costly metal, and in 1913 the search for a cheap substitute led to a copper-sheathed 43 per cent nickel-iron alloy, which is still widely used in the electrical industry. Today a wide range of different glasses and metals are fused together to form two main types of seal: *matched* seals, made with metals having the same thermal expansion as the glass being used; and *unmatched* seals, involving metals of different thermal expansion from the glass, but made extremely thin and in carefully designed shapes. Metals that have thermal expansion similar to those of certain glasses, and are used for matched seals, include tungsten, molybdenum, platinum, 50–50 nickel-iron alloy, and 26 per cent chromium-iron alloy. For unmatched seals, it is important that the metal used is ductile, and has a small cross-sectional area and a higher expansion coefficient than the glass. Copper is a notable example of a metal that is used to make unmatched seals; it may be sealed to almost any glass provided that the seal itself is correctly designed and made. The copper section of the component must be free to yield in order to prevent the glass cracking, and so it is usually employed in the shape of a hollow tube, cone, or disk, where the metal is thin enough to stretch without breaking when expansion occurs. The tungsten electric lamp is probably the most widely used light source. The bulb for this is produced on a high-speed automatic Corning ribbon machine, which is the most productive glass-forming machine in the world. In the smaller sizes, a single machine produces up to 2000 bulbs a minute. A ribbon of hot glass flows between rollers that leave circular depressions at regular intervals along the ribbon. This moves to a conveyor belt where molds rise around the depressions; compressed air nozzles drop down over them, puffing them into shape. After annealing, the inside of the bulbs can be frosted by spraying with an ammonium bifluoride solution to make them translucent.

Fluorescent lighting, first introduced in 1940, also depends on having a rigid, durable, and impermeable envelope, in this case a hollow glass tube. This holds mercury vapor at low pressure and under vacuum, through which an electrical discharge is passed. The radiation thus produced, when it comes into contact with the fluorescent powder coating on the inside of the tube, produces white light.

Neon lighting, too, uses a sealed length of glass tubing containing electrodes, and these in turn each consist of a metal cylinder encased in its own glass tube open at one end. The whole is then filled with an inert gas at $\frac{1}{50}$ atmospheric pressure, which glows when high voltage is impressed across the electrodes. Here again, only glass combines the qualities required for these tubes.

Sodium lamps, which are widely used for street lighting because of the excellent night visibility they provide, presented the glass-maker with a problem. Because of the intense chemical activity of the hot sodium vapor, sulfated glass proved inadequately resistant, and designers had to find a special chemical-resistant glass for the tube. Unfortunately the glass devised (which contained very little silica or alkali but large amounts of alumina and alkaline earth oxides) had poor weather resistance and was extremely expensive. For these reasons, sodium lamp envelopes consist of a thin layer of this glass sprayed or flashed onto the inside of a cheaper, more durable soda glass tube.

A further application of glass in lighting is in controlling the direction and intensity of both natural and artificial light. Shades, lenses, globes, and reflectors made of glass are extensively used wherever controlled lighting is a consideration. But perhaps the most valuable use of glass as a light reflector is the ingenious invention known as *cat's eyes*, which is now in use on roads throughout the world. A small glass reflector fixed in a cushion of rubber reflects the lights of oncoming traffic; the rubber cushion holding the reflector is merely depressed by wheels passing over it. Few modern applications of glass are so simple and yet so splendidly effective.

The suspension insulators used for high-voltage transmission and distribution cables across country require exceptional mechanical and electrical qualities. Special heat-resisting borosilicate glass is used where the voltage exceeds 17,500 V. Borosilicate glass is also used for the foundation of the lightning arresters fixed to the transmission and distribution cables, while liquid-filled power fuses and current-limiting resistors are also made from pressed cylindrical sections of borosilicate glass.

High-voltage insulators for power transmission lines must have great dielectric strength and enough mechanical strength to

The Corning ribbon machine. Finished bulb envelopes are transferred by a rotary transfer to the loading belt that takes them to the annealing lehr. Over 1000 domestic light-bulb envelopes can be produced per minute, while for smaller sizes rates of up to 2000 per minute are possible.

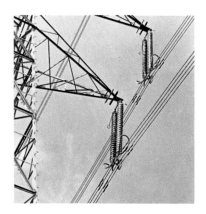

Glass suspension insulators on a 400-kV. power transmission line. Glass combines qualities of resistivity and mechanical strength that make it an ideal material for insulators of,this kind.

withstand the changing stresses caused by the effects of the wind on the cables. There are, too, many situations in which they are subjected to great temperature changes, both long and short term, as well as wide variations of humidity. High-voltage insulators can be made up in almost any size as a chain of identical or varied interlocking toughened-glass units. When a chain of these linked units is subjected to increasing tensile strain, it is the metal collar that fails rather than the toughened-glass unit to which it is joined.

Glass has played a significant part in the field of electronics. Glass tubing is widely used for valves and cathode-ray tubes, for pumping or exhausting valves, as material for all-glass bases, or for glass-to-metal seals. New compositions have been developed. Very fine copper wire (down to 1/1000 mm. diameter) sealed inside a fiber of glass to form an insulated conductor about the diameter of a human hair has wide application in miniature electronic circuits. Glass rods are used as resistors; some types of fixed capacitors use glass ribbon as the dielectric.

Glass also provides an excellent medium for the ultrasonic delay lines widely used in signal processing of many kinds, notably in radar, computers, and television. These tiny devices consist of a block of glass (high-purity silica is used because of its uniquely low attenuation of sound waves) of which two opposite faces are ground flat and parallel, with a transducer, in this case a thin plate of piezoelectric material, bonded to each face. An

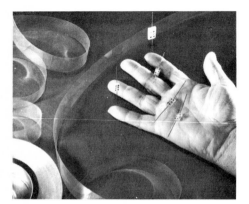

Flexible glass ribbon 0.025 mm. thick is used to provide the dielectric for some miniature fixed capacitors.

electric signal applied to one of these plates is converted to an acoustic shear wave that travels at reduced speed (compared to its speed as an electrical signal) through the block to the other transducer, where it is converted back to an electric signal. In this way electric signals may be delayed as required. The delay can be extended by using a multi-faced piece of glass such as the one illustrated on page 155, in which the mechanical wave is reflected many times inside the glass. Glass is an excellent medium because there is practically no loss due to absorption and because it is cheap. The effect of temperature change upon delay can be minimized by using glasses with especially low temperature coefficients. This application of glass will become more important as the speed of the logic elements used in computer and process control equipment is raised. Delay lines of this kind are also required in color television systems.

Many of the glass components required in electronics are miniature precision moldings. For making these, the methods of pressing glassware in molds by pouring molten glass direct from the forehearth (as described in Chapter 4) are too clumsy to be satisfactory. Two alternative processes are used for miniature moldings of this kind. One is molding from glass already drawn into a rod. The end of the rod is softened in a furnace and then formed between precision dies, giving clear, accurate moldings that are subsequently fire-finished. The second process is sintering, in which particles of finely ground glass are compressed into a coherent solid body. This cold-molding process can produce objects with intricate shapes and extremely accurate dimensions.

In the manufacture of sintered glass, dry finely powdered glass is mixed with a binding agent and pressed in fine-grained steel dies. The binder adds substance to the material during the preforming stage, and is then removed when the component is fire-finished. In the alternative slip-casting process, which is used for larger components, water is added to powdered glass to make a slip, or liquid, for casting. This is then poured into a plaster-of-paris mold, which absorbs most of the water. The casting is taken from the mold, dried, and fired at high temperature to give it mechanical strength. Both processes produce an extremely strong, nonporous, creamy white material from which radio coil forms, washers, and bearings are made. Sintered glassware can be made in various glass types for different purposes: 96 per cent silica glass, for example, is used for making molds for casting metals at temperatures of up to 1650°C.

Glass is sometimes used as a conductor of electrons instead of as an insulator. To achieve this, the outside of a tube of boro-

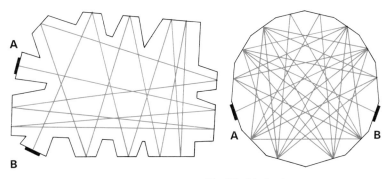

The 15-sided polygonal solid delay line in the photograph is made from 1-cm.-thick high-purity fused silica. The diagrams show typical folded paths between transducers (A and B) taken by the acoustic shear waves. High-purity silica is used because of its extremely low attenuation of such waves passing through it.

silicate glass is treated at high temperature with metallic oxides. These do not form a bonded layer but migrate a short distance into the glass, becoming an integral part of it, so that the surface of the glass becomes a conducting region that is colored blue by the tin and antimony oxides in it, but still transparent. Tubes of this kind are used as heating elements, mainly in specialized scientific applications where controlled heating is required, such as ion-exchange chromatography, zone melting, fractional distillation, and vacuum drying.

Domestic and Scientific Glassware

The packaging, building, engineering, and electrical industries are the four most important users of glass. No summary of commercial and industrial glass, however, would be complete without mention of two further types of glass products: domestic and scientific glassware. The first of these includes articles made of the three main types of glass—lead crystal, soda-lime, and the heat-resisting borosilicate glass originally devised for electrical purposes. Handmade lead crystal is probably the type of glass most readily associated with the term "domestic glassware," and the methods of making this largely luxury ware have already been described in Chapter 4. The refractive quality and the softness of this kind of glass make it particularly suited to the cutting and other decorative processes, and this more than any other part of the glassmaking industry is still within the rapidly shrink-

A selection of small, intricate components made of sintered glass. This process, in which finely ground glass is compressed into a solid body by cold-molding, offers an extremely high degree of dimensional accuracy, and can be used to form glass of any type.

Part of an acid cooler made of borosilicate glass. Acid flows through a series of pipes arranged one above the other, while cold water flows down the outside. There can be as much as 5 kilometers of glass pipe in a cooler of this kind.

ing province of the craftsman. The majority of domestic glassware, however, is made of soda-lime glass. This is cheap to produce and relatively easy to melt and form in large quantities by the automatic methods already described, since the bulk of glassware used in the home and by the catering trade is not much different in form from the containers used by the packaging industry, and the methods of manufacture are very similar. And, as in packaging, the postwar increase in both affluence and design consciousness have affected demand for the elegance and eye-appeal that glass can provide. The production of domestic glassware in Britain, for example, increased by 50 per cent between 1958 and 1964. In addition, the development of heat-resistant borosilicate glass has provided a wide range of oven and oven-to-table ware and added an entirely new dimension to the use of glass in the home.

Glass, with its chemical-resistant surface, is ideal for industrial piping, conveying a wide range of products from milk to hot acid, from magnesium to tomato juice. Toughened heat-resistant glass piping, which cannot harbor bacteria and whose transparency allows easy inspection, is vital in modern dairy farms, bottling plants, and heavy chemical industries.

Glass tubing is also used in heat exchangers. One of the most common methods of heating and cooling liquids in industry is to pass the liquids through a tube, or series of tubes, with a heating or cooling medium, usually water, on the outside. Glass would at first seem to be an unsuitable material for use in such equipment, because compared with metals it is a bad conductor of heat. However, the chemical inertness of glass makes it resist scale deposition much better than do most inexpensive metals.

A more spectacular use of glass is in the construction of industrial plant, especially in factories where chemicals are manufactured. It is very common to have chemical reactions or other processes, such as the separation of a mixture of liquids into its components by distillation, taking place in tall columns, and if the liquids are corrosive or if they must be kept very pure, these columns are made of glass. It is now possible to build glass towers up to 60 cm. in diameter, and of practically any height. An example of this use of glass is shown in the illustration on page 128. Not only the tower, but all the accessories, such as packings inside the tower, the pipes used for external connections, and even the circulating pumps, can be made of glass so that the liquid need not touch any other material at all.

All-glass towers are not used if the processes need to be carried out at high pressure, but it is sometimes possible to use metal vessels with glass linings instead. These are made by covering the metal wall with finely powdered glass and heating the vessel so that the glass melts and forms a continuous coating. The first layer is made of a type of glass that will bond firmly to the metal, and then up to five layers of a chemically resistant glass may be added to this.

The production of nonoptical scientific glassware has grown enormously during the last few decades. In 1935, production in Britain was valued at less than £300,000 ($840,000); in 1960 the figure was £4 million ($11,200,000). Production methods have developed to keep pace with the increased demand, particularly in cases where the product is manufactured at a bench by manipulating tubing in a gas-air or gas-oxygen blowpipe. Here the necessity for increased production has led to the application of mechanical aids. And although such aids can never completely replace the skillful bench worker, they can do much, not only to increase productivity, but also to improve dimensional and volumetric accuracy. This is an important consideration in a sector of the glassmaking industry where a high degree of accuracy is most vital—where, for example, a glass calorimeter thermometer is tested at every 0.5°C, to an accuracy of $\pm 0.002°$C. The rejection rate of such products as pipette blanks has been drastically reduced to around 5 per cent, as against 30–40 per cent when blanks were made by hand. The difficulty in this highly specialized corner of the glassmaking industry is that although the range of products required is very wide, the size of each individual order is often very small. For this reason complicated items have to be made up from a number of small components, the individual simplicity of which permits mechanical manufacture. For example, the manufacture of a complicated item such as a chemical condenser may be broken down in such a way that around 90 per cent of it is carried out mechanically. But so complex and specialized are the scientist's demands on the industry that a great deal of scientific glassware is still made by small firms producing bench-blown glassware by conventional craftsmanship. At the same time many research laboratories find it more convenient to run their own glassmaking department to satisfy their own special requirements.

The need for accurate scale markings on laboratory glassware exists wherever the article is to be used as a measuring device. Clinical thermometers, burettes, pipettes, and syringes are just a few examples of glass products that require such treatment. There are many ways in which the necessary calibration can be produced: It can be etched, engraved, or screen-printed on the glass, using methods already described in Chapter 4. But perhaps the most interesting method, because it combines the permanence of engraving with the simplicity of screen-printing, is the recently evolved diffusion method. Unlike the others, this method inscribes the markings in the actual substance of the glass. The process, first devised by Corning Glass, and called the Visu-red process, uses a copper-silver stain carried in a medium that makes possible printing by conventional screen methods After the printing, the marked article is fired in such a way that the silver and copper ions migrate into the glass to a depth that can be controlled by adjustment of time and temperature. After firing, when the residue has been washed from the surface, the markings remain as an integral part of the glass, and no amount of ordinary abrasion or washing will remove them.

Disks made of sintered glass, which has already been mentioned in this chapter, have important applications in the laboratory as chemical filters, either used separately or incorporated in standard or especially made laboratory glassware. Finely powdered glass is obtained by grinding down clean, thin-walled tubing in a glass-lined mill to avoid gathering metallic particles. The powder is then sieved with great care to the grain size required, molded without pressure in heat-resisting steel molds, and heated. The grains of glass powder become bonded to each other at sharp points and edges, which naturally melt first, joining together to make a minutely aerated, porous substance. The chemical inertia of the glass and the fact that it can be formed into a kind of porous cake by this method make it a perfect medium for a wide range of chemical filtration. Numerous grades of porosity are available, the finest of which will filter out particles two microns or less in diameter.

The Dewar vacuum flask is one glass product that has found valuable applications in both the home and the laboratory. It consists simply of two thin-walled glass containers, one inside the other and sealed at the neck. Three principles are involved: (1) the vacuum space between the two walls makes it impossible for loss of heat by *conduction* to occur by the direct route through the sides of the flask; (2) silvering of the vacuum-facing surfaces prevents heat loss by *radiation* because heat is simply reflected back into the vacuum-filled space; (3) the only appreciable heat loss still possible is by conduction *along* the inner wall and through the stopper, and this is kept at a minimum by the extreme thinness of the glass. In many laboratories vacuum jars are routinely used to store fluids at temperatures only a few degrees above absolute zero.

We have seen how the main industrial and commercial users

Right: Tight-fitting, tapered stoppers and joints ground to small dimensional tolerances are the most effective means of closing and joining laboratory glassware. Vacuum-tight sealing is achieved by the use of petroleum jelly, vacuum grease, or silicone greases.

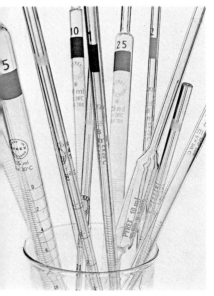

Left: laboratory glassware calibrated by the Visu-red diffusion method. A copper-silver stain graduation is applied to the surface of the article. This is then fired and the silver and copper ions migrate deeply into the glass.

Right: disks of sintered glass for use as chemical filters. The chemical inertness of the glass and the fact that it can be formed into a porous cake by the sintering process make it an ideal medium for a wide range of chemical filtration processes.

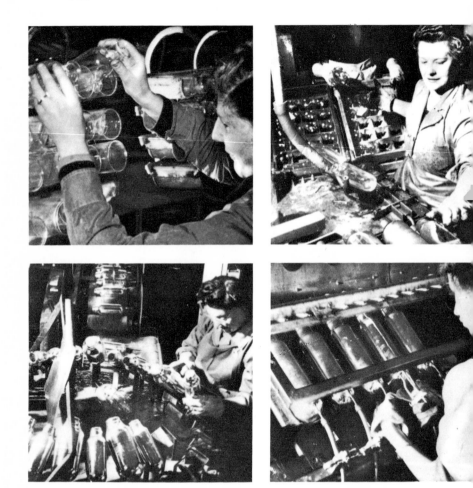

Four stages in the making of a domestic vacuum flask. Top left:
Assembling pairs of inner and outer thin-wall glass vessels. Asbestos pads
are glued to the outside of the inner vessel to serve as a support for the
outer vessel during manufacture. Top right: Filling the space between the two
vessels with silvering fluid. Bottom left: After silvering, the remaining
fluid is drained off and the silvered surfaces flushed with water. Bottom right:
Dried and heated vessels are finally connected by a tube to vacuum pumps
in order to exhaust the air from the inter-wall space, after which the space is
sealed, and the flask tested and placed in its canister.

take up the bulk of glass produced. Finally, let us glance briefly at some of the more unexpected and exotic jobs that glass is doing in industry today. In the steel mill, for example, not only does 96 per cent silica glass provide heat-resistant, corrosion-free surfaces for use at temperatures up to and sometimes above 1000°C, but glass is actually used as a lubricant. In the molding of both high- and low-carbon steels, glass powder, because of its low fluidity at extremely high temperatures, has been selected as the most practical lubricant for hot metal dies. Another surprising use of glass is in the oil industry, where toughened glass provides the perfect shell for encasing explosive charges for underground detonation, being the only material that, though strong enough to stand up to pressures of many hundreds of kg/cm^2, will disintegrate on explosion into a powder sufficiently fine to be harmless to delicate oil-pumping and other equipment. In the processing plants where synthetic textiles are made, glass wheels are used to pull rayon threads out of acid baths because glass is the only material that, while being impervious to the action of the acid, will not damage the rayon itself. Springs made of toughened glass have been flexed for millions of cycles without the work-hardening or fatigue that occurs in metals. Even in the field of surgery, thread spun from glass fiber is used for internal sewing work because glass offers a unique combination of strength, fineness, and resistance to the action of body fluids. Research has shown that the fibers are in no way harmful to the intestinal tract or to the bloodstream.

Considering the diverse and constantly increasing range of applications of glass in modern industry, it is not surprising that total glass production in the United States, for example, has more than quadrupled between 1900 and 1950, matched by a comparable increase in every industrialized European country. It is significant, too, that the biggest glass producer in the United States has more than 100,000 glass and glass-ceramic formulas on its files, each one combining properties that suit it to a specific job or range of jobs. Versatile, adaptable, offering an ever-widening range of sophisticated properties, glass provides modern technology with an indispensable tool.

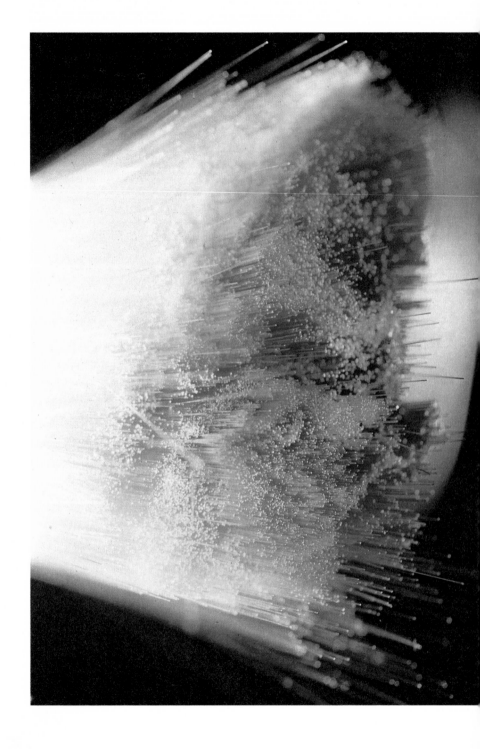

7 New Kinds and Uses of Glass

Glass is traditionally thought of as a rather weak, brittle material that breaks when unevenly heated but that has the virtue of being chemically inert. Some of its newest uses, however, are in jobs where it has to be strong, flexible, resistant to heat shock, and capable of being chemically machined. It is supposed to be transparent unless coloring materials are included in it, yet spectroscopic components are now being made out of a glass that is intrinsically colored. Glass has always been one of the best electrical insulators, yet it is now used as a source of electrons in channel multiplier tubes. These changes have been accompanied by, and are largely due to, a great advance in our understanding of the basic physics and chemistry of the material.

The great industries of the 19th century—mining, engineering, and textiles—were helped considerably by the related sciences. From the start of its existence, electrical engineering had a fruitful source of knowledge in pure research. The amorphous and chemically inert character of glass, however, made it seem a much

A loose bundle of sheathed optical fibers (×3). Each fiber transmits only the color incident on its other end.

less exciting subject for investigation than metals with their regular crystalline structure, and it was not until 1915 that the first university department of glass technology was started, at Sheffield, in England. World War I forced Britain and the United States to produce their own optical glass instead of importing it from Germany, and this greatly stimulated research into the properties of glass, as did the rising demand for hygienic packing materials and the spread of electric power resulting in a need for suitable lamp envelopes. The desire of glass manufacturers to improve their methods and to eliminate wasteful interruptions in production led to more investigations into the materials used as refractories, and their interaction with hot glass. One of the most important results of all this research is the knowledge we now have of the structures of different glasses, which was described in the first chapter. This knowledge makes possible the development of new kinds of glass, to be described in this chapter.

Photosensitive Glasses

Photosensitivity was first discovered in the so-called ruby glasses that are, in fact, clear, ruby-colored glasses owing their appearance to gold or copper inclusions. When these glasses are manufactured they are quite colorless at first, even when they have been cooled and become hard, and only develop their color if they are reheated to somewhere between their annealing temperature and their softening temperature. R. H. Dalton of the Corning Glass Works found in 1937 that if the glass is exposed to ultraviolet radiation while it is still cold the color it eventually acquires is deeper. As a result of this discovery, it is now possible to make photosensitive copper-ruby, gold-ruby, and silver-yellow glasses that do not acquire color at all on reheating unless they are first irradiated. If the ultraviolet light is made to pass through a suitable mask, such as a photographic negative, so that it strikes only certain areas of the glass, then only these areas will develop the color. In this way ruby and yellow patterns can be produced deep inside clear glass.

People have been arguing about what happens when a ruby glass is made for over a hundred years. The present belief is that when a compound of the coloring metal, such as gold, is added

Front and side views of photosensitive glass bars that have had seven progressively longer exposures.

to the glass batch, the metal dissolves as an ion and remains ionic even when the glass has hardened. On reheating, the ions are reduced to neutral atoms, which are insoluble in glass, and it is these that are responsible for the color. This controlled reduction is achieved by including in the batch oxides of polyvalent metals such as antimony, tin, or selenium, whose reduction potentials increase appreciably as the temperature decreases. In other words, at the melting temperature of glass they prefer to exist in states of high valence, but as the melt cools they give off oxygen, providing an oxidizing atmosphere that keeps the gold from being reduced. In this way the glass loses a lot of its oxygen, and on reheating to a low red heat the ions are slowly reduced and the atoms are able to move through the glass to coagulate into submicroscopic crystals that are too small to scatter light, but large enough to cause the selective absorption that produces color. A typical gold-ruby glass contains from 0.01 to 0.1 per cent of gold.

The new photosensitive glasses are different from the ordinary ruby glasses in that they contain none, or hardly any, of the polyvalent reducing agents. Instead they contain optical sensitizers, which become reducing agents after exposure to radiation. A typical sensitizer in gold-ruby glass is the trivalent cerium ion, Ce^{+++}, from which the radiation readily knocks out an electron, turning it into Ce^{++++}. While the glass is still cold, these electrons are believed to be trapped close to their parent ions. When it is heated and becomes less viscous they can move about and be captured by the gold ions to form gold atoms, which then coagulate. Roughly the same happens in copper and silver glasses, except that these metals can act as their own sensitizers; two Cu^+ ions turn into a neutral Cu atom and a Cu^{++} ion when the glass is irradiated and heated.

Surprisingly, this kind of glass has hardly been used at all for decorative purposes. It is possible to take ordinary photographs in photosensitive plate glass, but the chief use of photosensitivity is in marking scales or reticles in optical instruments. Very high resolving power is needed, which photosensitive marking can achieve because the image, unlike that in an ordinary silver halide film or plate, is essentially grainless. By cooling the glass at the appropriate time the size of the crystals is kept well below the wavelength of visible light.

S. D. Stookey, of the Corning laboratories, suggested an interesting application of photosensitivity in connection with opal glasses. These are opaque or translucent white glasses containing colloidal, usually crystalline, inclusions that scatter light. In a particular kind of opal glass the inclusions are crystals of sodium fluoride, and Stookey was interested to note that these, like the ruby glass, are clear when first cooled and only become opaque on reheating. At first he thought they might respond to ultra-violet light as well; in fact they did not, and the reason turned out to be that reheating plays quite a different role in these glasses

Fluid logic devices made out of photosensitive glass. The detailed pattern is first produced photographically, then developed by heat treatment, and finally etched out with acid to form fluid channels.

and has nothing to do with reducing agents. It is actually an example of temperature-controlled crystallization. Sodium fluoride crystals dissolve in the glass melt and remain dissolved as it cools. The solution eventually becomes supersaturated and crystal nuclei form, but this happens at such a low temperature that the glass is rigid and the molecules immobile. On reheating, the glass becomes less viscous, so that the molecules can move through it. As they migrate toward the nuclei, the crystals grow and the glass becomes opaque.

Stookey's idea was that it might be possible to make an opal glass photosensitive by including in the batch both sodium fluoride and the ingredients of a photosensitive ruby glass. The small metal crystals produced by irradiating and reheating might trigger the precipitation of sodium fluoride from the supersaturated solution and act as nuclei for the growth of sodium fluoride crystals. This was, in fact, possible; by choosing the right kind of glass and carefully controlling the heat treatment and the concentrations of the ingredients, an opal phase can be produced where the glass has been exposed, while the rest of the glass remains clear. For this to work, the glass must initially be very well melted to eliminate foreign bodies. These would act as nuclei for crystals to grow, whereas we only want those purposely provided by the sodium fluoride to be present. The north wall of the United Nations Assembly building has translucent windows made of opal glass with a marble pattern produced by this method.

This is the kind of glass that can be chemically machined. In the early days of television the problem arose of how an aperture mask could be made containing a quarter of a million small, precisely placed holes, and it was solved by using a photosensitive opal glass containing lithium silicate, in which the crystallized opal phase dissolves much more easily in hydrofluoric acid than the surrounding clear glass. Using ultraviolet light and a suitable mask, a three-dimensional photograph of the holes was produced in the glass. This photograph was developed by heating—that is, the opal phase appeared within the glass. Finally the holes were made by etching this phase out with acid. Up to 50,000 accurately positioned holes per square centimeter can be produced in glass in this fashion.

Electron micrographs showing the conversion of amorphous glass to crystalline glass ceramic (x 165,000). Left: a flake of essentially amorphous glass containing dissolved nucleating agents. Heat treatment produces nuclei that initiate the growth of crystals, shown as the dark spots in the center picture when they are 100 angstroms across. Right: Crystallization is almost complete with crystals now 600 angstroms across. Further treatment makes crystals coalesce into larger ones.

Glass Ceramics

In 1957 an accident led to the discovery of glass ceramic, a new strong material that is mainly crystalline and that is produced by a special kind of devitrification process. A photosensitive glass that has been irradiated was heated several hundred degrees above its usual developing temperature because of a fault in the furnace. Instead of melting it turned into an opaque, strong material—the first of the glass ceramics.

There are now many of these ceramics with a variety of uses, including the manufacture of missile nose cones. These require special properties of strength, transmission of radar waves, and resistance to thermal shock and to rain erosion at supersonic speeds. Domestic ovenware made from glass ceramic is marketed under the name Pyroceram in the United States and as Pyrosil in Great Britain. This ovenware can be taken straight from the icebox to the top of a red-hot burner. Typical glass ceramics are 40 per cent harder than borosilicate glass, with flexural strengths of up to 3500 kg/cm^2.

Glass ceramics are made by what is essentially a process of controlled devitrification. Unlike the products of ordinary devitrification, however, the crystals are very small (one micron or less across), very uniformly distributed, and free from pores or voids. The material is from 70 to 100 per cent crystalline, the rest being glass, and is strong because the crystals are so small, strong, and well-bonded. If a surface flaw occurs, does

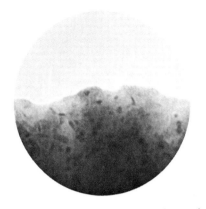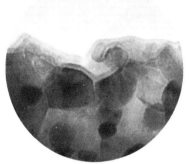

not propagate readily through so many crystal boundaries.

In the accidental discovery of glass ceramics, the initial nucleation was caused by ultraviolet light. Nowadays special catalysts or nucleating agents are used, which are dissolved in the molten glass and which readily precipitate at the appropriate temperature when the glass is cooled, forming billions of crystal centers per cubic millimeter. These act as seeds for the subsequent devitrification when the glass is reheated, and ideally should have an atomic structure closely similar to that of the crystal being nucleated.

When a glass-ceramic object is made it is always formed as an ordinary glass article and only then cooled and reheated. The fact that the devitrification takes place after the article is formed means that a strong, opaque, ceramic object can be made by conventional glass-forming methods, and can be ground, polished, and visually inspected for internal defects before finishing. Unlike ordinary ceramics, glass ceramics are non-porous and they generally have greater strength and scratch resistance.

By choosing the right chemical composition for the glass batch, these ceramics can be made to have special mechanical, thermal, or electrical properties. For instance, the strength of glass ceramics means that they generally stand up well to heat shock, but for exceptionally good heat-resisting qualities they are made from crystals, such as beta-spodumene or beta-eucryptite,

Fire and ice being used to show the resistance of a glass-ceramic dish to thermal shock.

that have an extremely low expansion coefficient. This means that a temperature change will produce very little stress in the material.

Beta-eucryptite glass ceramic has some interesting properties. The crystals, which are in fact lithium aluminum silicate, can be made so small that they do not scatter light, giving a glass ceramic that is completely transparent. Beta-eucryptite has an open atomic structure with an unusual spiral geometry, with the result that its expansion coefficient is not only small but negative,

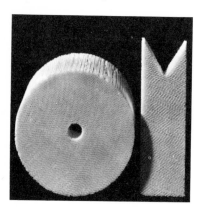

Glass ceramics can be made into thin-walled cellular structures, used for making gaseous heat exchangers and infrared burner plates.

so that this kind of glass ceramic shrinks when it is heated; we shall see how this fact is used in the chemical toughening of glass.

Chemically Toughened Glass

We have already seen how toughened glass can be made by prestressing it, so that the skin is in a state of compression. The standard way of doing this is by chill tempering, or suddenly cooling the glass. However, the same effect can be achieved by various methods in which the surface layer is given a different composition from the rest of the glass, and this process, which is called chemical toughening, gives glass a flexural strength that may be as high as 7000 kg/cm^2.

One method of chemical toughening is to form the required article from a glass containing lithium oxide and then immerse it in molten sodium chloride. Some of the lithium ions that are moving about near the surface will escape and be replaced by sodium ions, and as the glass cools these cause considerable stresses in the surface because they are much larger than the lithium ions that they replace. In this process, which is called ion exchange, the number of sodium ions entering is the same as the number of lithium ions leaving, so that the glass remains electrically neutral.

Another method is to give the glass a surface layer of low-expansion glass ceramic. Paradoxically, the standard way of doing this is to use ion exchange of the reverse kind to that just described, that is, to let lithium ions displace sodium ions in the glass. The starting material is a soda-alumina-titania-silica glass, and when sodium has been replaced by lithium, the basic ingredients of beta-eucryptite are present. Titania happens to be a good nucleating agent for this crystal, and the subsequent heat treatment ends with a skin of glass ceramic being grown at high temperature. As we saw earlier, beta-eucryptite has a negative coefficient of expansion. When the glass is finally cooled, therefore, its surface tries to expand while the inside tries to shrink and a system of stresses is set up similar to that in chill-tempered glass.

As with glass ceramics, the final strengthening treatment is always applied after the article has been fabricated and finished, and may leave it either opaque or transparent, depending on the process. Like chill-tempered glass, these toughened glasses may shatter completely to harmless pieces if broken, provided that the compression layer is thick enough and the internal tension high enough. Chemical toughening is expensive, but has advantages over thermal toughening. It gives strengths two or three times as great, it can be applied to thin glass and to articles of complicated shape, and heating does not irreversibly destroy the

Chemically toughened glass can be bent. When it is released it goes back to its original shape. Glass of this kind can be given a flexural strength that may be as high as 7000 kg/cm².

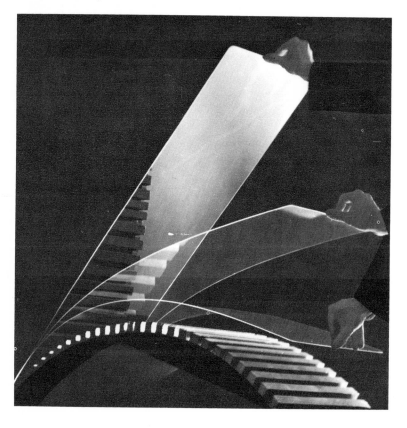

effect. Perhaps the last word in strong glass at the moment is Pyroceram that has been chemically toughened, giving a material whose flexural strength is 17,000 kg/cm^2.

Photochromic glass

We have described several processes in this chapter that depend on controlled nucleation and arrested crystallization. Glass is an ideal medium for this, since the crystals can be held at any stage of their growth simply by cooling the glass, and when it is re-heated for the crystals to grow they remain dispersed throughout the material. Photochromic glass is one of the most recent uses of the technique.

Photochromism has been known for nearly a century; it is the phenomenon of certain materials darkening when exposed to sunlight or other suitable electromagnetic radiation, and regaining their original color when radiation is switched off. There are several hundred photochromic compounds known, with a number of different mechanisms taking place in them to produce the effect. Basically, however, they all involve atoms or molecules that are *bistable*—that is, that can exist in two states having different atomic, molecular, or electronic configurations. In their normal state the molecules are colorless, but when light shines on them they switch over to the other state, in which they are colored. In the absence of light, they revert to their original state.

Photochromic liquids have been used to paint dolls, which therefore tan in the sunlight and lighten again indoors. Other potential applications for photochromism are in self-adjusting sunglasses, sunshields, or windows, for aircraft windshields that are intended to protect pilots from the flash radiations of a nuclear explosion, and as memories in optical data-storage devices. Until recently, however, there was little practical progress because all the devices made suffered from fatigue when taken through several cycles of darkening and clearing. The photochemical processes taking place produce some highly reactive chemicals that react irreversibly with oxygen, or with moisture, or with other chemicals present, thus removing some of the photochromic material and eventually causing the device to lose its effectiveness.

Photochromic glass darkens when exposed to ultraviolet rays and clears when the ultraviolet is switched off. This photograph shows the time taken for the darkening and clearing. The darkening, as in photographic film, is due to silver halides. Unlike the photographic process, however, the action is reversible.

Corning have now produced photochromic glass in which this problem has been overcome. Specimens of this glass have been exposed outdoors, day and night, for more than two years, and to thousands of cycles indoors, with no noticeable fading. The photochromism is due to dispersed crystals of colloidal silver halides (chlorides, bromides, iodides, or mixtures of these). They are precipitated from the melt during cooling and reheating, and thus can be made extremely small, about 50 A across, and with concentrations as low as 1 part in 2000 by volume.

The wavelengths that cause darkening depend on the chemical composition of the glass. Silver chloride glasses are sensitive to the violet or ultraviolet region of the spectrum, while adding the bromide or iodide takes the sensitivity into the visible region. The special silver chloride glasses that are darkened only by ultraviolet light have an interesting property—fading of the color is accelerated by visible light. Conversely, these glasses are darkened more quickly by ultraviolet alone than by mixed ultraviolet and visible radiation. In other words, visible radiation produces "optical bleaching," which competes with the darkening process. Increasing the temperature generally has the effect of discouraging the coloring of any of these photochromic glasses.

The coloring is believed to be due to the formation of neutral silver atoms, just as in ordinary photographic film. The radiation frees an electron from the chloride ion and this electron is then captured by the silver. The important difference is that the darkening in photochromic glass is reversible, and this is believed to be for two reasons. The first is the extremely small size of the crystals; the volume of a crystal in a photographic emulsion is about 60 million times as great, which encourages the neutral silver atoms to aggregate into stable colloid particles. The second reason is the nature of glass. It is impermeable, which means that the neutral chlorine atoms do not diffuse away from the reaction zone, as they do in a film, and it is nonreactive, so that the silver and chlorine are not removed by other reactions. The actual composition of the base glass is, of course, important in this respect, and the ones that seem to be best are alkali borosilicates. It is the nature of the glass, also, that prevents fatigue, by preventing diffusion of the silver and chlorine and protecting them from the atmosphere.

The main difference between photochromic glass and photosensitive silver glass is that in the one the silver ions are part of silver halide crystals, while in the other they are dissolved in the glass. The process in a photosensitive glass is irreversible because once an electron has been freed it is firmly trapped at a site and it stays there even when the ultraviolet is switched off.

Glass that Conducts Electrons

Glass that conducts electricity is not new. Most commercial glasses contain ions (such as sodium ions, Na^+) that carry charge. If a glass is being used for its conducting properties, however, ionic conductivity has disadvantages; for instance, if a direct current is passed through it for any length of time the ions migrate toward the appropriate electrodes. The glass thus becomes polarized and its resistance goes up.

In the last few years, glasses have been made with electrons as carriers of current. The term "electronically conducting glass" has occasionally been used for the kind of glass described in Chapter 6, in which the surface layer has special properties that make it conduct electronically, but what we are referring to now is bulk electronic conduction, which is something more revolutionary. The new type of glass is sometimes called *semiconducting* glass, and the name is appropriate: Its resistivity is typically from 10^4 to 10^{12} ohm-cm., which is between those of a good insulator and a good conductor; the resistivity decreases with temperature; and the conduction apparently takes place by a mechanism like that in conventional semiconductors.

The semiconducting glasses all contain multivalent elements as part of the glass structure, and most of them do not contain silicon. A typical example is the system $P_2O_5 - V_2O_5$ in which vanadium is the multivalent element and the role of the phosphorus pentoxide is to help the formation of a glass. We believe that the glass is actually deficient in oxygen and so some vanadium is reduced to the 4-valent state. This means that there are V^{4+} and V^{5+} ions present, the latter having lost one electron more than the former. Conduction takes place by the transfer of an electron from one kind of ion to the other so that they exchange their degrees of ionization, electrons hopping from ion to ion throughout the glass.

Another glass of this type is made from a mixture of arsenic selenide and arsenic telluride, $As_2Se_3 - As_2Te_3$, in which selenium and tellurium are multivalent semiconductors. This is an example of a glass that contains neither silicon nor oxygen, which are usually regarded as the main ingredients of the material. For most applications they are less useful than oxide glasses because of their low softening temperatures.

The most important use of the semiconducting oxide glasses so far is for making channel electron multipliers. These are hollow tubes, about 50 mm. long and 1 mm. wide on the inside, that are used for detecting extremely low concentrations of electrons. For instance, they have been fitted to space vehicles and used to measure the density of electrons in the aurora.

The way in which such a tube works is shown in the diagram on page 179. The potential drop has two effects: It keeps a current flowing in the glass tube, so that there is a supply of fairly energetic electrons that can easily be knocked out of the glass altogether; and it supplies an electric field that accelerates an electron once it has been knocked out. When a single electron from space enters the tube on the left and hits the glass, it knocks out several more. These in turn do the same, so that about 10^8 or 10^9 electrons finally emerge from the other end; the current, in effect, has been amplified about a hundred million times. On

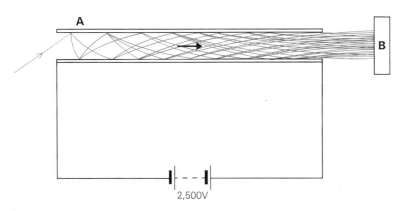

A channel multiplier tube made of semiconducting glass. When a single electron hits the glass, it knocks others out (A), so that finally 10^8 or 10^9 electrons emerge from the tube and reach the detector (B). The voltage between the ends of the tube produces a current of free electrons, ready to be knocked out, and a field that accelerates those that do leave the glass.

emerging, this number of electrons can be detected and measured by devices that would not have responded to the initial, single electron.

A tube of this kind will respond to X-rays as well, since these can also knock out electrons, and so it is useful for detecting low intensities of X-rays. More interesting, a bundle of parallel tubes can be used to intensify an image. X-rays can form images in the same way as light waves, and an image intensifier of this kind improves their visibility and contrast.

Glass is not the only material from which electron-multiplying devices can be made, but it is especially useful because it can be drawn into fine tubes, and the exact value of its resistivity can be adjusted precisely by using the right concentration of the multivalent ingredient.

The system As_2Se_3–As_2Te_3 mentioned earlier is one of a family of glasses made from the sulfides, selenides, and tellurides of the arsenic group of metals, and referred to collectively as *chalcogenide* glasses. Like oxide glasses, some of them are insulators and others semiconducting, and in fact the oldest of them, arsenictrisulphide glass, which was known in 1870, is a dielectric. All of

Arsenic trisulfide glass. This is used for making optical components for infra-red spectroscopy, and windows that let infrared waves through. The photograph shows lenses and, at the bottom, a disk of the material.

them are colored, and the ones that are semiconducting are completely opaque to ordinary light.

All of these glasses, on the other hand, transmit infrared light. Ordinary glass contains metal-oxide bonds that prevent it from transmitting wavelengths very far into the infrared. Chalcogenide glasses are free from these bonds and are therefore used to make prisms and lenses for use in infrared spectroscopy and to make windows for radiation pyrometers. There are other materials that are used for these purposes, but either they are very expensive, like germanium or sapphire, or they are substances such as potassium chloride that are easily attacked by chemicals in the atmosphere.

Fiber Optics

A solid tube of refractive material such as glass can transmit light over considerable distances and round curved paths, using the phenomenon of total internal reflection, which was explained in Chapter 2 (see diagram opposite). A thick glass cylinder can thus transmit light around corners, but an image, such as a pattern of light and shade, focused onto one end, will be seen at the other only as an area of roughly uniform intensity, which is an average of the intensities of the light falling on different parts of the transmitting end.

The situation is transformed if, instead of a single thick cylinder, a bundle of fine fibers is used. Each fiber transmits only the

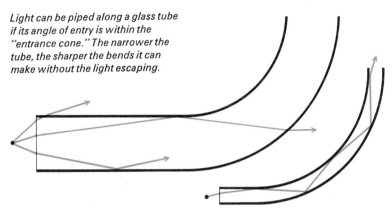

Light can be piped along a glass tube if its angle of entry is within the "entrance cone." The narrower the tube, the sharper the bends it can make without the light escaping.

light falling on it, so if the fibers are properly aligned, occupying the same relative positions at each end of the bundle, an image can be transmitted whose grain will be the area of a single fiber. We say that the bundle transmits as many bits of "information" as there are fibers in it. Such a bundle can be made flexible, and because the fibers are so thin, can be bent around very sharp corners. Moreover it will be much stronger than the rod; the breaking stress for a fiber 0.025 mm. in diameter can be as great as 8000 kg/cm^2.

In 1926 John Logie Baird toyed with the idea of transmitting an image by means of such a bundle of fibers, each one transmitting a tiny portion of the whole image. In the 1930s, flexible· fiber optics were used by surgeons, not to transmit an image, but to send light into regions inside the body. For a long time, however, little progress was made with an image-transmitting device because of the problems of light loss. If two fibers are touching each other, light will pass from one to the other instead of being reflected. A scratch in the outer surface of a fiber will alter the shape of the interface at that point so that light will strike it at too sharp an angle and will escape. Electrostatically attracted dust particles around a fiber will scatter light, because during the process of reflection it penetrates about half a wavelength into the medium of lower refractive index. Finger grease on the surface will cause a change of critical angle at the interface.

A major advance in overcoming these problems was made in

the early 1950s when A. C. S. van Heel in the Netherlands and B. O'Brien in the United States recognized that the fibers can be made nearly leak-proof by sheathing them in glass of lower refractive index than the fiber core itself so that most of the reflections take place at the protected interface of the two glasses, rather than at the exposed surface of the fiber itself. To make such a fiber, a rod of highly refracting glass is surrounded by a tube of less strongly refracting glass and the two are softened and drawn together. One of the main difficulties in manufacture is finding pairs of glasses that have not only precisely specified refractive indexes, but also compatible softening points, viscosities, and expansion coefficients, so that the drawing process is possible. Formerly, flexible light guides were usually made from Perspex or similar materials, and it is mainly the stringent conditions necessary for producing a sheathed fiber that make glass the preferred material today.

There are two main kinds of image-transmitting fiber optic. The first, called a *fiberscope*, is a bundle of long fibers sealed together at both ends, and is like a flexible light guide except that the fibers have to be aligned. This is achieved by winding them onto a groove in a large drum until the bundle reaches the desired cross section and then slicing it across. If the ends of the fibers are properly sealed together the face of the optic can be treated as a single piece of glass and polished to produce a good optical finish.

To give a picture of good resolution, the fibers should be as narrow as possible. Theoretically, the diameter must not be less than a few times the wavelength of light, but this is not a limit of practical concern. The difficulty about making fibers very thin is that they become weak and hard to see, and their usual diameter in a light guide is about 0.05 mm. This is not good enough for a high-quality fiberscope and to improve on it, several fibers that have been drawn to a diameter of about 0.25 mm. are held together and drawn a second time as a group. This gives a multiple fiber consisting of individual fibers embedded in a core of sheath glass, the diameter of a core being as little as five microns (0.005 mm.). These multiple fibers can be wound onto a drum just as single fibers can, in order to make a fiberscope, and they can be produced with square or hexagonal cross sections that can be packed more closely than round fibers, to eliminate dead space. The snag about this process is that it is slow and very expensive.

The second kind of image-transmitting device is called a fused fiber optic, and is made by stacking several multiple fibers together and fusing them into a solid mass. It is inflexible and a few inches long, compared to several feet for a fiberscope. Solid optics are essentially optical instruments. They can be made with tapered ends, so that the diameter of each fiber is reduced in the same proportion, and will then magnify or diminish an image. One or both faces can be made curved, and the optic used to compensate for the field curvature that results from lens aberrations. Solid optics in which the cross sections at the two ends have different shapes are also made and used, for example, to convert the circular image of a star into the size and shape of the collimator slit in a spectrometer. In this way a spectral analysis can be made using all the light received from the star.

Fiber optics have found applications in many fields. In medicine they are being used for viewing inside the human body, where their flexibility gives them an advantage over conventional endoscopes because it allows greater penetration with less discomfort to the patient. Fused optics are chiefly used as faceplates for cathode-ray tubes where it is required to take a photograph of the trace on the screen. In the ordinary way this is quite difficult, first because design means that the end of the tube bulges outward so that the camera is looking at an awkwardly curved object, secondly because the light from the tube is emitted at all angles so that the camera lens can only trap a little of it—the light output is especially low if the event being recorded is a very fast one, as is often the case—and thirdly because some light is reflected inside the glass of the screen and strikes the phosphor a second time. The diagram on page 184 shows how a fiber optic can cure all of these faults at once. Such a plate may contain 70 million fibers, and special manufacturing problems are created because it has to be airtight in order to preserve the vacuum inside the tube.

Some fiber optics are made now in which each fiber is clad in

Above: a flexible fiberscope with the transmitted image shown enlarged. Below: a fused fiber optic. Because the optic is tapered the image is magnified or diminished, depending on the way the optic is used.

Below: A cathode-ray tube of conventional design (A) and with a fiberboard faceplate (B). In A the trace on the screen is being photographed with a camera. Most of the light misses the lens, contrast is made poor by reflections within the screen, and only part of the screen is in focus. In B a photographic plate is pressed up against the fiberboard and these faults are absent.

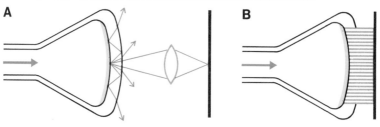

a dark glass that absorbs light. These give improved contrast because light cannot stray from one fiber to the next, and are especially useful as faceplates for cathode-ray tubes that have to be viewed in a brightly-lit room. The ambient light is normally scattered back into the room by the phosphor screen, but with the fiber optic faceplate much of it is absorbed by the cladding. This type of cladding is known in the United States as extramural absorption (ema).

An exotic use that has been suggested for fiber optics is the sending of secret messages. If the fibers are deliberately scrambled, the picture transmitted will appear meaningless. A photograph made by contact with the emergent face could be decoded with the aid of a twin of the original optic. The optic and its twin could be made by taking a fiberscope with the fibers properly aligned at either end, braiding them in the middle, and cutting it in half.

Glass in Modern Technology

Many of the most interesting applications for glass today make use of its traditional properties in new scientific and technological devices, and to round off this survey of modern developments we shall mention a few of these.

The first is in the making of lasers. A laser is an instrument that produces a very powerful, coherent beam of light of a particular wavelength when it is stimulated by light of the same wavelength. It does this because it contains certain atoms or ions in excited states, which respond to the stimulus by emitting more light of the same wavelength in phase with the original beam. One type of laser is made out of glass that is doped with neodymium ions, Nd^{+++}. It is very useful to be able to make glass lasers, as opposed to the ruby lasers that existed before them, first because glass can be produced with a very high optical quality, and secondly because there is a limit to the size to which useful ruby crystals can be grown. Since glass is a good solvent and is transparent, it may seem surprising that glass lasers were not made first. The difficulty is that when ions are dissolved in glass their electronic energy levels, which are important to the laser action, are seriously affected by the glass material itself.

This photograph shows the very high optical quality of laser glass. Sighting is along a 50-centimeter rod of the glass, at the other end of which is a man holding a similar rod.

Chromium ions, for example, which give ruby its characteristic red color and are responsible for the laser action, give a green color when dissolved in glass; this change in wavelength is due to the modified properties of the electrons. Neodymium is special because the laser action is not due to the outermost electrons but to electrons belonging to an inner shell that is largely immune to the influence of the glass material, provided it is a silicate glass. The glass must not contain iron, which absorbs light of the wavelength in question.

Glass is also being used in new ways in electronics. One of the latest advances in this field is the production of microcircuits—complete, fairly complicated circuits laid down on a background, or substrate, one or two centimeters square. The circuits are made from very thin films of metal or insulating material: A resistor might be a metal line a few thousandths of a centimeter wide. Transistors or diodes in the form of tiny chips of semiconducting materials can also be added. The substrates must be of a material that is electrically insulating, smooth enough for the circuit to be continuous, and able to dissipate the heat generated. Substrates are usually made out of glass or ceramic; glass gives a smoother surface but ceramics dissipate heat better. To get the best of both worlds a very useful substrate has been made by glazing a ceramic. The new glass-ceramic materials described earlier in this chapter are now also being used as substrates for miniature circuits.

A much older use for glass is in making optical filters. By giving them the right composition, glasses can be made to absorb chosen wavelengths in the electromagnetic spectrum while letting others through. Traditionally this is done by including colored ions as a solution in the glass, but controlled nucleation processes, of the same kind as are used in making glass ceramics, have given us a new method. The German firm Schott, of Mainz, is making a glass that stops visible light but allows the infrared through. The visible wavelengths are absorbed by submicroscopic crystals of appropriate composition in the glass itself. It is, of course, only the near infrared that is transmitted; as we have already seen, ordinary glass absorbs the wavelengths in the far infrared.

We already know that ordinary glass is weak under tension but not under compression. Its high compressive strength is put to use in deep-sea research, where it is used for making deep-diving vessels and other protective housings. Glass ceramics and toughened glass are also used, but for structures that are more or less permanently submerged, ordinary borosilicate glass will often do, provided the structure is shaped so that the glass experiences a uniform compressive stress. A spherical hull made of glass materials has a working depth of more than 10,000 m. compared with 1400 m. for steel and 4500 m. for aluminum.

In industries and laboratories where nuclear power is used,

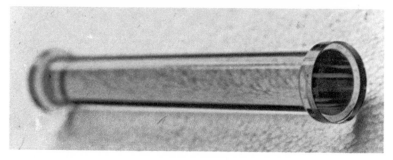

Top: an opened-up laser unit. The farther of the two tubes is the neodymium glass rod surrounded by a water jacket, and the nearer is a flashtube for raising the neodymium ions to an excited state. The lower photograph shows a neodymium glass rod by itself.

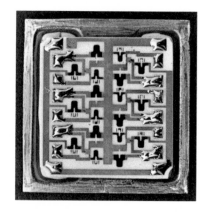

Right: A microcircuit laid down on a glazed ceramic. Resistors (black) are thin films of tin oxide, with the resistance values precisely adjusted by etching some tin oxide away, producing the white lines that protrude into the black areas. The six small squares are transistor chips, and the connections between the circuit elements are thin films of gold. The whole circuit is in a metal tray 2.5 cm. square. The 16 blobs of solder show where 16 connecting pins protrude backward through the metal tray.

glass that has a high lead content and that therefore absorbs harmful gamma-rays is used for viewing-windows. Silver-phosphate glass is used to make radiation dosimeters, small "badges" worn as safety devices by people working with the nuclear materials. Silver-phosphate glass normally contains a large amount of silver in the ionic state, Ag^+, and the gamma-rays release electrons that reduce it to the neutral metal, much as in the photosensitive silver glasses. Now the neutral silver atoms will fluoresce when exposed to ultraviolet radiation, but the ions will not. To measure the radiation dose, therefore, the badge is irradiated with ultraviolet and the amount of fluorescence observed is a measure of the number of silver atoms in the glass.

We have seen how the traditional properties of glass are being put to new uses, and also how it can be given quite new and unexpected ones. Science, technology, and industry depend heavily on the materials that they can use, and research can improve the properties of these materials in three ways—in degree, in versatility, and in precision. We may need a substance that has a greater strength or that can be more accurately shaped than any existing substance; we may want a material that combines several quite different properties; or we may want to control the magnitude of a particular property very precisely. In the last fifty years glass has been improved in all these ways. Before World War I it was used almost entirely for its optical qualities and chemical resistance, while today its range of useful properties is so great that it is taking over many of the functions once performed by other materials. Almost the only useful property of metals that glass cannot be given is ductility, which would mean that a break need not be as catastrophic as it is now. Perhaps we shall succeed in making ductile glass one day. In any case, it is certain that glass is today, and in the future will be even more, an essential part of life in an age of technology.

Index

Note: Numbers in *italics* refer to illustrations and captions to illustrations.

Abbe, Ernst, 114, 115
achromatic doublet, 110, *111*, 113, *116*
Adams, 97
Agricola, Georg, 59, 79
Alhazen, 112
aluminoborosilicate glass, 41, 42
aluminum, 22
ammonium bifluoride, 104, 151
angles: of deviation, *37*; of incidence, 36; of refraction, 36
annealing, 96–8, 118
antimony, 54, ·78, 167
Aristophanes, *The Clouds*, 112
arsenic, 22, 78; trisulfide, 22, *180*; selenide, 178, 179
Ashley, William, 68
automatic tube-drawing process, *88*

Baird, John Logie, 181
barium crown glass, *116*, 119
Bausch and Lomb, 115
Bénédictus, Edouard, 143
beryllium, 22
beta-eucryptite, 172
beta-spodumene, 172
Bicheroux process, 91
Bontemps, Georges, 114
boron, 22
borosilicate crown glass, 39, 42, *128*, 147, 152, 155, 157
bottlemaking, *67*, 68, 71, *82*, 83, *84*, 86, *96*, 130–5
bottling unit, *132*
brick, states of a, *14*
bubbles, 78–9, 114
building blocks, preformed hollow glass, 136–7, *137*

cadmium, 22
calcium: carbonate, 78; metasilicate, 78
cast glass, *see* rolled glass
ceramics, 170–2, *170*, *172*
cerium oxide, *108*, *121*
chalcogenide glass, 179–80
Chance Brothers, 114
channel multiplier, 178
Chérubin d'Orléans, Père, 112, 117
chromatic aberrations, 109–12, 113, 114

cladding, glass, 138
cobalt, 54
conductivity of glass, *see* glass, electrical properties of
configurational contraction and expansion, 24–7, *26*, 31, 43, 96, 97, 99
continuous-casting process, *92*, 107
continuous filament yarn, *95*; *see also* glass, fiber
copper, 150; oxide, 54, 55; wheel engraving, *105*
Corning: Glass Works, 115, 147, 159, 166, 168; ribbon machine, 107, 151, *152*
corrosion, resistance of glass to, 40–1
cristallo, 58
cristobalite, 18
crown glass, *63*, 113, *116*
Crystal Palace, London, 70, *70*
crystallization, 15, 16, 17, 169, *170*
cullet (waste glass), 74
curve generator, *120*
cut glass, *105*; *see also* lead, crystal
cylinder-blown glass, 68–9, 70

Dalton, R. H., 166
de la Bastie, 99
deformation by viscous flow, *17*
devitrification, *9*, 10, 32, 170
dispersion, 38–9, *39*, 109–10; partial, 111; relative, 111, *111*
Dollond, John, 113
Dutch glass, *61*

Eastman Kodak Company, *116*
Egyptian glass, 50–4, *50*
electromagnetic spectrum, 22
electron tubes, 43
electronically conducting glass, 177–9, *179*
electronics, 153–5

Faraday, Michael, 114, 119
ferrous oxide, 145
fiber, *see* glass, fiber
fiberscope, 182, *184*, 185
fictive temperature of glass, 26–7
flat-drawn process, *88*, *89*
flat glass, 54, 63–5, 68–9, *69*, 77, *88*, *89*, 89–94

flint glass, 39, 113, 114, *116*
float glass, 92–4, *93*, *106*
fluorescent lighting, 151
foam glass, 140–1
forming processes in glassmaking, 71, 79, 80–6, *81*, *82*, *84*
Fraunhofer, Joseph, 114, 127
Fresnel lenses, 127, *127*
fuels used in glassmaking, 75–6
furnace, *58*, 60, *60*; regenerative continuous, 71, 74, *74*, *75*, 76, *76*, 77; 16th-century, *58*
fused fiber optic, 183, *184*
fused quartz (fused silica), 19

germanium, 22
glass: blowing, 79, *80*; chemical stability of, 40–1; commercial and industrial uses of, 129–63; electrical properties of, 42–3, 148, 153–5, 177–9, *179*; fiber, 30, 31, 32, 94–5, *94*, 130, 138–9, *138*, 145–6, *147*; fiber optics, *165*, 180–5; grinding and polishing, *121*, 124–6; inspection for defects, 107; mechanical properties of, 29–32; methods of production of, 73–107, 117–24; thermal properties of, 23, *25*, 41–2; types and composition of, 43–7; wool, *see* glass, fiber
glass-formers, 18–22
glass technology, first university department of, 166
goblets, *57*, *61*, *62*
Goerz Dagor, 115, *116*
greenhouses, *140*, 141–2
Guinand, Pierre Louis, 114, 118

Hall, Chester Moor, 113
heat-resistant ovenware, *72*, *85*
helium, 38, 148
Herschel, Sir John, 114
Hood, H. P., 147
hydrofluoric acid, 40, 69, 103, *105*, 169
hydrogen, 39, 148

infrared light rays, 22, 33, 145, 180, 187
infrared spectroscopy, *180*
insulating properties of glass, *see* glass, electrical properties of

insulation, double-glass, 137, *140*
insulators: high-voltage, 152; suspension, 152, *153*

laminated safety glass, 100–3, *102*, 143–4
lasers, 185–6, *186*
lead: crystal glass, 65–7, *66*; oxide, 22, 114
lenses, *see* optical, glass
lime, 20, 22, 59, 74
lithium, 31, 115; oxide, 172, 173; silicate, 169
Lucite, 22

manganese, 54, 56, 58; dioxide, 56
Manzini, *Dioptrica Pratica*, 118
marble bushing process, *95*
melting process, 73–9
metallic oxides, 20–2, *48*, 54, 55, 104, 156
metastable state of liquids, *see* supercooling
microcircuits, 187, *188*
microscopes, 114–5, 126
Moody, B. E., *Packaging in Glass*, 135
Morey, G. W., 115, *116*
mosaic, glass, *52*, 55, 142
Mount Palomar, telescope, 127

neodymium glass rod, *188*
neon lighting, 151
Newton, Isaac, 38, 113
Nordberg, N. E., 147

O'Brien, B., 182
opal glass, 168
optical: filters, 187; flat, 126; glass, 109–27
Owens, Michael, 68

Paxton, Sir Joseph, 70
Perspex, 22
phosphorus, 22
photochromic glass, 175–7, *176*
photography, 115, *116*
photosensitive glasses, 166–9, *167*, *168*, 177
Pilkingtons of Great Britain, 91, 107, *141*, 142

Pittsburgh Plate Glass Company, 115
plate glass, 69, 91; polished, 91
platinum, 119, 150
polarized light, *9, 29*, 39, 75, *133*
Porta, Baptista, 112
potash, 59
prisms, *39*, 119–24, *123*, 126
Pyrex glassware, 42; *see also* toughened
  glass
Pyroceram, 170
Pyrosil, 170

quartz, 18, *19*, 20

radiation dosimeter, 189
rare-earth oxides, 115
refraction, 36–9, *36, 38*
refractive index, *35, 36*, 37, 38, 39, *39, 116,* 119
rolled glass, 90–2
Roman glass, 50–4, *52, 53*
ruby glass, 166–7
Rupert of the Rhine, Prince, 99
Rupert's drops, 99, *101*

Saint-Gobain glassworks, *65*
Saint Sophia, church of (Constantinople), 55
sand, 18, 59, 74
sandblasting, 104
Schott, Otto, 115, *116*
Schott (Mainz), 119, 187
scientific glassware, 158–9, *161*
sheet glass, *see* flat glass
silica glass, 40, 42, 78, 148; 96 per cent, 42, 147, 162
silicon dioxide, 18, 20, 21, 22, 148
silver: chloride, 55, 176; halides, 166, 167
sintered glass, 154, *156*, 160, *161*
soda, 20, 59, 74
sodium, 38; carbonate, 78; chloride, 31; fluoride, 169; hydroxide, 40; lighting, 151; sulfate, 78
specific heat: of glass, 26; of water, 12
stained glass, *48*, 54, 55, 142
Stookey, S. D., 168
strain pattern in glass, *29*
sulfated glass, 135

sulfur, 22; dioxide, 135; trioxide, 135
sulfuric acid, 103
supercooling, 13–8

thermal toughening of glass, *see* toughened glass
thorium, 22
Tiberius, Emperor, 98
tin oxide, 54, 58, 167, *188*
titanium, 22, 131
Titanizing process, 131
total internal reflection, 37, *38*, 180
toughened glass, 31, *31*, 42, 98–100, *101*, 143–4; chemically, 173–5, *174*
transformation temperature of glass, 23–7, 31, 96, 97, 99
transparency of glass, 32–5
Triplex Safety Glass of Gt. Britain, *143*
tube drawing glass, 87
tungsten electric lighting, 151
two-way mirrors, 140
types and composition of glass, *see* glass, types and composition of

ultraviolet light rays, 22, 33, 145, 166, 169, 189
United Nations building, 169

vacuum flask, Dewar, 160, *162*
van Heel, A.C.S., 182
vanadium, 22
Venetian glass, *56*, 57–8, 59, *61, 68*
vinal, 102, *102*, 144
viscosity, 16, 17, 18, 20, 25, 27, 42
Visu-red process, 159

Warren, 19
water glass (soda-silica glass), 40
Williamson, 97
windshields, *see* laminated safety glass
wired and figured glass, *see* rolled glass
Wood, John, 143

X-rays, 179

Zachariasen, 19
Zeiss, Carl, 114, 115; Protar, *116*
zinc, 22
zirconium, 22